THE LOST HISTORY OF
BALLINDALLOCH
Balfron

A M M and S M O Stephen

with Drawings and Heraldry by S M O S

FRONT COVER

Ballindalloch House by SMOS 1977 and Heraldic shields (from left to right)
of Lennox, Drummond, Fleming, Cunningham, Cooper and Stephen

BALLINDALLOCH

The estate is private and personally maintained so owner's
permission should be obtained by anyone desiring access.

First published in 2009 by
A M M and S M O Stephen
Cutty Cottage, Station Road,
Balfron, Stirlingshire G63 0SX

ISBN: 978-0-9562013-0-0

Designed and typeset by Mark Blackadder

Printed and bound by the MPG Books Group in the UK.

THE LOST HISTORY OF
BALLINDALLOCH
Balfron

Ballindalloch House. Watercolour by John Gubbins 1987

Contents

Acknowledgements

This creation of ours has taken so long to produce we feared it might never happen. Now we would like to thank the people in Balfron and beyond who have helped to make Ballindalloch a happy place, and especially those who have enabled us to write a book about it.

Without the expertise of Lorna Maine, Stirling Council Archaeologist, there would have been no tale to tell, and without the kind advice of Richard Drew this volume might never have got into print. We are deeply indebted to the families of Cunninghams, Coopers, Donaldsons and Glens for all the pictures and information they have provided. Countless requests and inquiries have been answered by exceedingly helpful curators and librarians in Glasgow, Edinburgh, Stirling and Kilbimie in addition to Carol Murphy at the library in Balfron.

Alisoun Grant's advice on heraldry and Liz Arthur's guidance on costume design have been invaluable, while Rosemary Reid-Kay, Fiona Robertson and our daughter-in-law Trix have helped to iron out literary gaffes. During the early stages our son, Graham, made a huge contribution by giving his time and computer skills.

Although it is not possible to name everyone who has helped and encouraged us we hope that each of them will now accept our enormous gratitude.

This book is dedicated to our family
and all the people who love Ballindalloch

Introduction

In the year 2003 the people of Balfron decided to commemorate the 700th anniversary of our village, the earliest reference being the Charter of Inchaffrey in 1303.[1] To celebrate this milestone in local history, a series of special events was arranged, and we were glad to host a garden fete which came to be known as 'The Funday'.

Apart from having the biggest back garden in Balfron, Ballindalloch was an appropriate venue, having been for centuries the Big Hoose of our village. As Ballindalloch Castle had ceased to exist, few were aware that it had, from mediaeval times, been the centre of local administration, justice and employment. Because Balfron and Ballindalloch were interdependent this story belongs to both.

While celebrations were being prepared we learned that Ballindalloch's history spanned about 4,000 years because our house was standing on the site of a Bronze Age burial mound. This surprising piece of news gave rise to our own contri-bution to the fete in the form of a small exhibition entitled 'The Lost History of Ballindalloch'. The interest shown in our hurried presentation encouraged us to write this book.

There would have been more information to share if the historian, John Guthrie Smith, had not died suddenly in 1894 before completing *Strathendrick and its Inhabitants from Early Times*. Although this invaluable work was eventually published, the chapter on the Cunninghams of Ballindalloch, which he had intended to include, is sadly missing.[2]

We now contribute our own inexpert findings, hoping in a small way to complement *The Balfron Heritage* written by our local historian Jim Thomson. Though ours is only a light-hearted history we hope you will find interest and enjoyment among these pages.

Sandy and Sue Stephen,
Balfron, 2009

Ballindalloch Old House

CHAPTER I

THE VANISHING TOWER
and THE MYSTERY MOUND

When Sandy and Sue Stephen brought their family to Ballindalloch in 1976, they found themselves with a large Victorian pile amidst glorious surroundings, but they knew nothing at all about its history. Interest was awakened when John Glen, who sold them the property, kindly gave them a framed picture of Ballindalloch Old House. It was in fact a monochrome photograph of a painting which was said to have been made by a member of the Cooper family. The Coopers had owned the estate for 120 years and their house had been portrayed before it was demolished and replaced by the Mansion House which was built for them in 1868. Nobody knew what had happened to the painting and the Old House had long since gone, but was believed to have stood somewhere between the existing house and the stables.

Life at Ballindalloch brought many surprises. The summer of 1977 turned out to be unusually dry and traces of old foundations appeared on the front lawn. The outlines of buildings corresponded with the house in the picture and an aged oak with forked branches was recognised from one shown in the picture. Kay Cameron was keenly interested in local history and came to inspect the evidence which confirmed the site of the Old House. As a former Donaldson of Ballindalloch she knew the place well and was able to impart more information by telling the Stephens that there had once been a castle at Ballindalloch. This news was tantalising because she did not know where the castle had stood and no picture of it seemed to have survived, but there could be no doubt about its existence because Sandy and Sue soon discovered that 'Ballindalloch Castle', variously spelt, featured consistently on early maps of Stirlingshire.

The Old House in the picture looked suitably ancient and typically Scottish, being harled with a slated roof and crow-step gables. It was an ungainly, three-storey building with gabled dormers, and Lshaped, with a two-storey wing which appeared to have been added. An incongruous looking gable jutted awkwardly above the join, and the wing itself looked odd because, instead of being constructed at right angles to the main building, it appeared to be slightly splayed. Sandy and Sue began to wonder if the artist had got it wrong.

Through mutual friends the Stephens were able to get in touch with descendants of the Coopers. Some of their family had settled in Australia and the first contacts were Robert and Jeanette Minter in Sydney. Jeanette's grandfather had been the last Cooper to own the Ballindalloch Estate. She and Rob came to stay and were remarkably polite on finding that the Stephens had drastically altered their ancestral home. After that there were friendly visits from several Cooper descendants. They supplied much information but nobody could identify the site of Ballindalloch Castle.

The Minters sent a copy of the Sale Brochure, printed in 1922 when the Cooper family had sold Ballindalloch to Norman Donaldson. The brochure said 'An ancient tower and fortalice[1] stood here, which was demolished when the present Mansion was built in 1868' and went on to say 'When workmen were digging the foundations of the new Mansion a large tumulus was laid open and a number of urns of a pre-Roman period found containing bones and ashes'. But once again, nobody knew the site of

the tumulus, let alone the fate of those interesting relics.

Sandy and Sue Stephen puzzled over the missing tumulus but while their house was undergoing major alterations, historical research was not a top priority. Two decades went by before they acquired a copy of the 1861 ordnance survey map which confirmed the position and orientation of the Old House. The map also showed a mysterious round enclosure at the place where the Mansion House was destined to be built seven years later. The site was an obvious vantage point, so the Stephens began to think this unexplained feature on the map might have been the missing castle as the information on the brochure was frustratingly unclear.

Early in 2003 Sue was planting a tree by the burn, when her spade struck masonry. It seemed like part of an old building or a wall, and again the castle came to mind. She made phone calls and eventually tracked down Lorna Maine, the Stirling Council Archaeologist. Lorna came to investigate and, though Sue's 'find' turned out to be a red herring, the visit produced surprising revelations. When Lorna was shown the picture of Ballindalloch Old House she exclaimed 'There is your castle' and then explained why. Old Scottish castles, known also as Tower Houses, were fortified by solid stone walls topped with high battlemented towers, but when times became more settled and defences were no longer needed, many redundant towers were reduced in height.

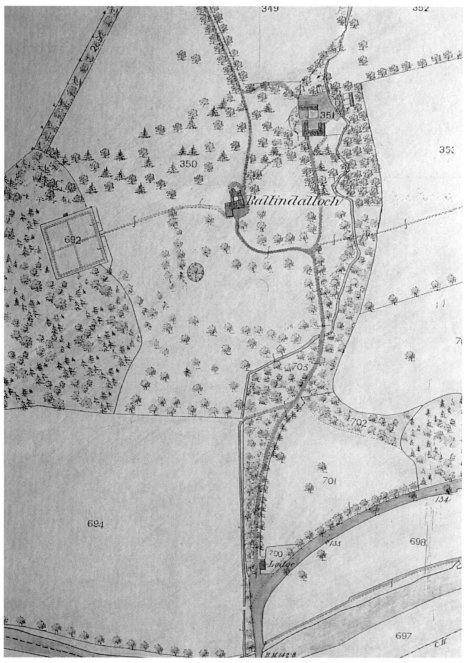

Detail from Ordnance Survey Map of 1861 showing the Old House with Home Farm and Stables to NE, and Burial Mound to SW (reproduced by permission of the Trustees of the National Library of Scotland)

The Estate of Ballindalloch

THIS beautiful and attractive Estate, extending to 642 acres, lies in the Valley of Strathendrick in the Western Division of the County of Stirling, within easy reach of Glasgow, Loch Lomond, and the Trossachs.

The MANSION HOUSE is a modern and commodious structure, and is picturesquely situated within extensive and finely-timbered Policies and Parks. The river Endrick skirts the grounds.

The distinctive feature of the property is its special suitability for a gentleman engaged in business in Glasgow, and desirous of having a country residence within easy reach of the city by train or motor car. For many years the house has been let to such tenants. It is situated about a mile from Balfron Station on the Forth and Clyde Railway (North British system), and about 19 miles from Glasgow by rail and road. Balfron village is about half a mile distant from the House, where there are medical men, churches, and a post, telegraph, and telephone office.

Historically the Estate is of considerable interest. Formerly the property of the Earls of Glencairn, the lands of Ballindalloch, with a considerable tract of the surrounding country, had for long been a free Barony previous to their re-erection into a Barony by James II. in 1687, and the Superiority of this Barony, and the privileges attaching to it, go with the property to this day. An ancient tower and fortalice stood here, which was demolished when the present Mansion was built in 1868. The site of the former edifice is marked by an old sundial, which is an antiquarian curiosity, and is illustrated and described in Dr Ross's "Ancient Sundials of Scotland." The property lies in Rob Roy's country, and the Clachan of Aberfoyle is in the neighbourhood. When workmen were digging the foundations of the new Mansion a large tumulus was laid open and a number of urns of a pre-Roman period found containing bones and ashes.

In the event of the proposed Ship Canal through Scotland, *via* Loch Lomond, being constructed, it is anticipated that its route will lie through two of the Farms on the property, but as these are at a distance from the Mansion House the amenity of the place will in no respect be adversely affected.

Sale Brochure 1922 (Messrs Cooper & Brodie, WS, Edinburgh)

Doors and windows were added and wings built to provide more comfort and space. This had happened to Ballindalloch Castle and that odd looking gable on the Old House had been part of the fortified tower.

The elusive castle had been traced at last and the picture was there to prove it, but the information which followed was even more intriguing. The 'pre Roman' artefacts turned out to have been far older than expected and evidence confirmed them to have been approaching 4,000 years old. Having studied the Sale Brochure and the old ordnance map, Lorna was able to identify the circular enclosure and deduce that the Victorian

Mansion had been built directly over the site of a Bronze Age tumulus. The ancient burial mound measured approximately 23 metres in diameter and could have dated from around 2,000 BC. The Ballindalloch tumulus had never been recorded among the archaeological sites in Stirlingshire but this omission has now been rectified.[2]

Spurred by these discoveries, Sandy and Sue became extremely interested in the Bronze Age and their investigations also turned to castles. A sub section of Sod's Law states that if one wishes to examine anything on a map, half of it is on one page and half on another. The 1861 survey splits the outline of Ballindalloch Old House neatly between two sheets,

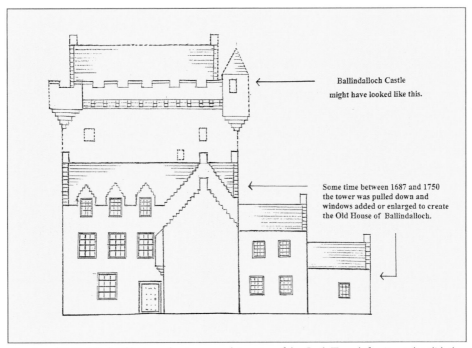

Ballindalloch Castle might have looked like this.

Some time between 1687 and 1750 the tower was pulled down and windows added or enlarged to create the Old House of Ballindalloch.

Elevation of Ballindalloch Old House showing a speculative view of the Castle Tower before it was demolished.

Aiket Castle after reconstruction (courtesy of Robert and Katrina Clow)

making accurate measurement difficult, but the tower appears to have measured 16 x 8 metres. The added wing may have been angled to give a more generous aspect as this peculiar splayed arrangement had also been applied to Kinneil House at Bo'ness.

From Guthrie Smith's history of Strathendrick the Stephens learned that the Cunninghams, who became Earls of Glencairn, had been owners of Ballindalloch, so they were glad to meet Robert and Katrina Clow, who had rescued and restored a similar Cunningham stronghold, Aiket Castle in Ayrshire. Though Ballindalloch Castle had ceased

to exist, these two tower houses could have been built around the same time. The earliest record of Aiket was 1479 when Alexander Cunningham received his charter of lands five miles from the Cunningham headquarters at Kilmaurs. The Aiket tower measures 22 x 11 metres and was built to replace an earlier one.

According to a volume of *Stirlingshire Place Names* compiled by the Reverend William Nimmo, 'Balinodalach' was first recorded in 1238. Early fortifications were constructed from wood, most of the stone castles built at that time being Crown property.[3] Though it is not known what structure existed then, by the 16th century

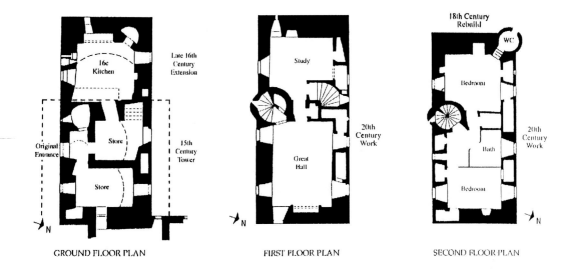

Floor plan of Aiket Castle

Ballindalloch was considered to rank among the important castles of Scotland. The cartographer Timothy Pont undertook the first inland survey of Scotland in the 1590s. On his maps stylised castles were depicted and the significance of each one was indicated by the number of turrets. On his map of Lennox, Ballindalloch achieved top rank with three turrets, and one of his maps of Scotland shows only five places in West Sterlinshyr – Duntraith, Gartnefs, Fintray, Touch and Balnadalach. Pont's survey was published by Blaeu in 1662.[4]

Though it is not known when the Ballindalloch tower was reduced, it proba-bly happened during the 18th century because the castle was still intact in 1687 when John Cunningham of Drumbeg received a Charter which included 'the tower and fortalice'. Although a tower might be destroyed by cannon power it could still provide refuge during the feuds of rival landowners. As late as 1777 the Rev. William Nimmo complained about the owners of 'thofe caftles', lamenting that 'Conftant difcord with their neigh-bours obliged them to hold their houfes always in a ftate of defence'.[5]

Recycling is nothing new. After Ballindalloch tower was reduced the stone would almost certainly have been re-used

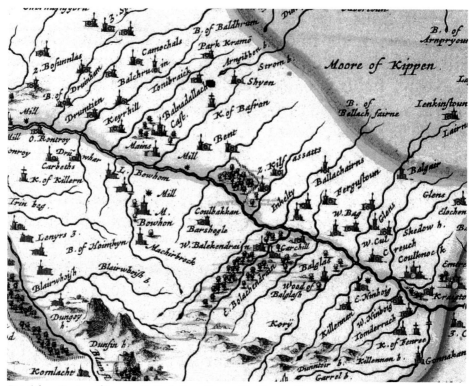

Detail from Province of Lennox, Scotia Antiqva. Surveyed by Timothy Pont c.1595

to build the added wing. Then, when the Old House was demolished, redundant stone was used to back the walls of the new mansion. The blocks of red sandstone can still be seen in the Ruin Garden.

When the Stephens were altering their house Sue was amazed to discover a fine Georgian grate boarded up in a small attic room. It deserved a better home and was duly relocated in their entrance hall to welcome guests with a glowing fire on winter evenings. They could not imagine why an old Georgian fireplace had been built into the nursery pantry of a new Victorian house, till their cousin Mary

Dunlop suggested the Coopers had brought it from the Old House. It was built with hobs which could be used for boiling kettles to heat baby food. Sandy and Sue had wondered why their yellow pine doors were typically Victorian, each with four panels, whereas those in the old servants' quarters were of red pine, and made in the Georgian style, with six. Then they realised the doors in the service area must also have come from the Old House. It is good to know that these relics from the past are still in use, and old stone from Ballindalloch Castle still forms part of the present Ballindalloch House.

CHAPTER 2

THE BRONZE AGE

Today Ballindalloch is a small estate of some 80 acres on a sheltered slope just west of Balfron. To the south lie the Campsie Fells where two shadowy craters are all that remain of primeval eruptions which once shook this earth. Untold ages came and went before the advent of mankind, but about 4,000 years ago, there was an organised settlement in what is now the parish of Balfron.

The Bronze Age is the name of a period roughly between 2,000 and 450 BC when bronze was the best metal alloy known to man. Although it belongs between the Stone Age and the Iron Age, varying rates of development caused these 'Ages' to overlap. When the last Ice Age drew to a close around 8000 BC, Britain had not yet become an island. Nomadic tribes followed wild herds which had crossed by land from continental Europe and as the ice receded they hunted and gathered food, gradually penetrating the virgin territory which is now Great Britain. Eventually the nomads abandoned their wandering life, settled in permanent homes and began to farm. This story begins with the Bronze Age because of the evidence found at Ballindalloch.

Prehistoric Ancestors

When early settlers staked their claims on the banks of the Endrick they started to mould the raw landscape into the farmland of today. Over the centuries invaders plundered and dynasties rose and fell but agriculture continued. The land was worked to feed the population and passed from father to son through the generations. Today there are Balfron families whose forebears have farmed in the area for hundreds of years and some of them may have ancestors who were living in Strathendrick during the Bronze Age, or even before.

The Village of Weeping

Though Balfron is normally a cheerful place its name comes from the Gaelic 'bail-a-bhroin' said to mean 'the village of

weeping'. According to tradition a terrible disaster occurred here long ago when wolves still lurked among the forests. Unsuspecting villagers are said to have come home one day to discover that hungry wolves had gobbled up their children. Although there have been other interpretations the sad tale lives on. That woeful lapse in child care still serves as a warning while the image of the Balfron Wolf proclaims the need for vigilance, having been thoughtfully embroidered on a table-cloth of the Women's Rural Institute.

The Homestead by the Water Meadow

Ballindalloch means 'the homestead by the water meadow'. Old Stirlingshire documents and maps record also Balinodalach, Bandalloch and Balnadallach. Translating from the Gaelic, Bal means – town, hamlet or homestead; dall – dale or field; och – water meadow or haugh field. The name is shared by other places near rivers with fields which flood. In Perthshire two

neighbouring Ballindalloch farms have haugh fields on the river Lednock, and the well known Ballindalloch Castle in Banff is on the edge of a big haugh by the Spey. At the Stirlingshire Ballindalloch the Endrick can still burst its banks and deluge the haugh till the pastures look more like the Mississippi.

Burial Mound / Barrow / Cairn / Tumulus

Each of these names means a mound. A cairn is a mound made of stone but cairns and tumuli do not relate exclusively to burial. 'Long barrows' were also used for burials but most of the Stirlingshire barrows are round. The largest is at Doune with a diameter of 34 metres. The Ballindalloch Barrow as shown on the map measures approximately 23 metres. Having withstood the passing of ages, this venerable mound was destroyed by Victorians who seemed unaware of its age or significance, even though its place in ancient history belonged to an epoch shared by Stonehenge, the Trojan Wars and Abraham's journey to the Promised Land.[1]

A barrow contained a central burial chamber or chambers, constructed from stone or wood with a low, narrow passage to provide access. This was covered with stones, or with earth, which is thought to have been the case at Ballindalloch. The barrow is likely to have been an important burial place made for a local chieftain or warrior. Members of his family were probably included and subsequent generations could also have been buried there.

Within living memory a stone cairn measuring 9 metres across, still existed at Cairnhall Farm on the moorland north of Balfron, but in 1969 it was demolished.[2] To pagans gazing out to the distant hills, it would have seemed a fitting place to enter eternity.

Sacred Rites

Ancient cults and superstitions still survive among people who worship inanimate objects, and call on supernatural powers by performing extraordinary rituals to seek fertility, prosperity, power and enlightenment. Customs of disfigurement with body piercing and skin dyes also continue to exist.

Half a mile north of Ballindalloch the land rises to a gentle summit known as the 'Ibert' which means the 'Place of Sacrifice'. Only the name survives. The site, which now forms part of Station Road, could once command views in every direction and provide a high place to observe the night skies and draw near to the spirits above. A sacrifice could be followed by ceremonial feasting. So far, no evidence of human offerings has been found in Balfron, though some tribes have, in surprisingly recent times, continued to indulge the practice of devouring their victims.

Decent Burial

The occupants of the Ballindalloch Barrow would have been cremated on a funeral pyre before their bones were

Ballindalloch Barrow

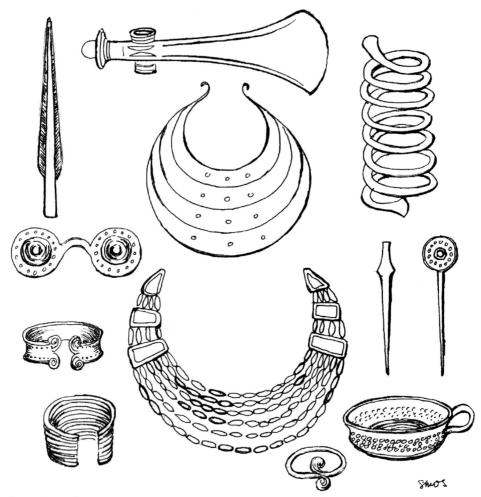

Bronze Age artefacts

placed in large urns for final interment within the mound. Bronze Age burials could take place with or without cremation. When preparing for the afterlife, pagans liked to take possessions with them so grave goods included jewellery, weapons, tools and utensils.[3] Nobody knows what became of the Ballindalloch urns or the bones inside them, let alone

what treasure might once have lain in the mound. Local museums have no knowledge of the find, but strange things lurk in attics so an ancient relic might still turn up.

Artefacts from Bronze Age burials have provided information about people who departed fully clothed or even armed. Splendid adornments allowed the wearers to enter the next world not only looking their best, but also proclaiming rank and office.[4] Heroes were given celebrity treatment. Though no report of a Bronze Age funeral at Ballindalloch has reached us, this extract from The Iliad gives Homer's version of an ancient tale which could have been contemporary.[5]

Dawn came once more, lighting the east with rosy hands, and saw the people flocking together at illustrious Hector's pyre. When all had arrived and the gathering was complete, they began by quenching the fire with sparkling wine in all parts of the pyre that the flames had reached. Then Hector's brothers and comrades-in-arms collected his white bones, lamenting as they worked, with many a big tear running down their cheeks. They took the bones, wrapped them in soft purple cloths and put them in a golden chest. The chest they quickly lowered into a hollow grave, which they covered with a layer of large stones closely set together. Then hastily they made the barrow, posting sentinels all round, in case the bronze-clad Achaeans would attack before the time agreed. When they had piled up the mound, they went back to Troy, foregathered again and enjoyed a splendid banquet in the palace of King Priam, nursling of Zeus.

'The Beaker People'

The so called 'pre-Roman urns' in the Ballindalloch Barrow would have been

Urns – also known as Beakers

Bronze Age cinerary urns. These were used exclusively for burials and could stand up to 50 centimetres high to accommodate an entire human skeleton.[6] The urns were made of clay and decorated with rows of grooves and indentations. Similar vessels in various sizes were used for domestic purposes and archaeologists refer to them all as 'Beakers'. Examples from the Bronze Age have been found all over Europe, and often among grave goods at burial sites. For many years experts attributed the beakers in Britain to a tribe of immigrants who were spuriously named 'The Beaker People'.[7] This theory has been rejected and itinerant craftsmen are now believed to have introduced the beaker technology from the continent.

As clay is plentiful round Balfron, beakers could have been manufactured locally, but a cinerary urn would have been difficult to make and therefore expensive. The potter's wheel had not yet been invented so great skill was required to coil the clay in layers to the required height and then fire this very large vessel. Being interred in a prestigious cinerary urn was probably beyond the means of ordinary folk so the occupants of the Ballindalloch Barrow seem to have been high ranking people.[8]

The Bronze Age Way of Life

Our early forbears were organised people though our knowledge of their lives is limited.

The general picture is one of tribal groups in a structured territorial society ruled by chiefs and holy men. Scattered farmsteads were occupied by extended families whose wealth and livelihood were based on stock rearing and agriculture. Livestock included cattle, sheep, pigs and goats so crops were enclosed by hedges or fences.

Bronze Age dress code

Houses were circular and wood framed with mud walls and thatched roofs.[9] The occupants wore fur and leather as well as linen and woollens which had various fastenings and were patterned with coloured dyes. Meals were cooked on a central hearth. Hedgehog, barley bread and nettle pudding could have featured on the menu while wild garlic, which still grows along the burn and the verges on Station Road, was cultivated in early times and may have flavoured many a stew.

Beyond the pastoral areas of Strathen-

drick a sprawling forest of oak and pine was interspersed with clumps of alder, willow, hazel and birch. Ballindalloch Moor and the Campsie Fells would have provided a hunting ground with red deer, wild boar and brown bear, not to mention those notorious wolves. Traps would have been used as well as spears and arrows. For the human race, life was tough and the death rate high. Infections were hard to treat and serious wounds were usually fatal. Survival depended on being fit. Many children died in infancy and few adults lived beyond the age of forty.[10]

Prehistoric houses

Specialised tools were made from stone, flint, horn and bone as well as bronze which was smelted with tin from Cornwall and copper from Wales. Bronze-smiths travelled widely. Flint came from the south of England and amber from the Baltic. There were gold mines in Ireland and also in Perthshire at Tyndrum, but before coins were made early trade was done by barter.

The climate is said to have been warmer and drier so the course and level of the Endrick probably varied. Without dams, the winter rain may have made the floods more frequent and last longer than they do today. Timber tracks could be laid across bogs and, when overland travel was laborious, water could offer a better alternative. The Endrick could be fished with nets and harpoons from small craft made with animal hide. Primitive dug-out canoes were made from hollowed tree trunks and could be lashed together to transport loads. Even then, foreign trade was taking place because during the Bronze Age seagoing ships already existed and could follow coastal routes to the Mediterranean.[11]

TEENAGE FASHION IN THE BRONZE AGE
When Egtved Girl was discovered in Denmark her crop top, belt and cord mini skirt had survived in her hollowed tree coffin for about 3,400 years.

This Desirable Residence

The Ballindalloch Barrow would have served as a landmark for people crossing the river. Today there is a bridge on the A875 where there once was a ford. From the bridge, the main road bends sharply eastward on its way into Balfron, while Ballindalloch avenue continues straight ahead and follows the course of the Clachan Burn directly to the Stables. By continuing north, this route might, at one time, have led to the Clachan of Balfron.

The Stables of the old Home Farm, enjoy an ideal location looking south to the Campsies. Today the property has instant appeal and back in the Bronze Age it would have been equally desirable with fertile pastures in a warm, sheltered hollow and a constant water supply from the burn. At one time, proximity to the Barrow might have held particular significance. As successive dwellings would have been built on this unusually desirable spot, it could have been continuously occupied for 4,000 years.

CHAPTER 3

THE DARK AGES
OF BALLINDALLOCH

After the Balfron tumuli were built there is a distinct lack of evidence regarding what happened for almost 2000 years. During this murky period in prehistory the way of life may not have changed that much when our forebears lamented that things were not what they used to be back in the good old Stone Age. But the way of death altered when Barrow building fell from favour and individual burials came to be preferred. The occupants of stone cists could be laid to rest either flat or folded and, for the well-to-do, cremation and grave goods continued to be desirable options.

From 2000 to 1000 BC development was gradual as the inhabitants of Strathendrick tilled the soil and tended their herds, with cereal yields improving and stock rearing giving better returns. Farmed animals became a more reliable source of food than hunting. Pack animals came into general use and labouring locals must have been thankful when oxen replaced manpower for ploughing the

land. The wheel reached Britain around 1300 BC but probably took some time to trundle its way to Strathendrick.

The Iron Age

Big changes began after 500 BC when iron smelting came to Britain. The new technique had been discovered in Asia Minor around 900 BC, by the Hittites who guarded their secret as long as they could. In Scotland iron ore was plentiful along with a good supply of charcoal to produce the high temperature required for smelting. Technology advanced because iron was superior and more versatile than bronze for manufacturing tools, weapons and agricultural implements. As well as being harder, tougher and sharper the iron could be beaten into shape. About 75 BC the wheeled plough came to Britain from the Continent. This revolutionary piece of equipment was used for breaking up loams and clay, as well as clearing woodland for agricultural development, so it might have been useful for working the

Tribal warrior

heavy soil in Strathendrick.

During the last millennium BC the British climate took a turn for the worse. Cold wet weather had a detrimental effect on areas where fertile land was turned to bog. Fresh fields were sought when meadows became marshes and over-worked soil was exhausted.[1] The population had increased, causing competition over possession and when intruders presented a threat, local inhabitants had to protect themselves and their property. In Scotland stone brochs and duns were built

and these were later followed by timber crannogs on lochs. Most dwellings continued to be circular and roofed with thatch.[2] Tribal groups began to congregate in 'hill forts' which were actually small towns protected by ditches and palisades.[3] The stone walls of Dunmore Fort at Fintry enclosed an area the size of a football pitch with space for numerous dwellings.[4] Each community was governed by a chief and in the social hierarchy a warrior class emerged. In the course of time tribal units combined to form regional divisions which grew into minor kingdoms.

The Roman Occupation

For almost four centuries Britain formed part of the Roman Empire. Though Julius Caesar landed in 55 BC, it was almost a hundred years before the invaders began to colonise England. In 79 AD Agricola marched on Scotland to subjugate the northern tribes and he named their territory Caledonia. North of the Central Lowlands he built a series of 'Glenblocker' forts, including Drumquhassle near Drymen, Malling on the Lake of Menteith, Callander and Doune. Agricola's forces continued north to Aberdeenshire and defeated the Caledonians at Mons Graupus, but his campaign was cut short when his army was recalled to the Danube. He may have been thankful because his son-in-law Tacitus recorded, 'The climate of Britain is objectionable with its frequent squalls and showers'. Roman soldiers were used to warmer climes and the weather reduced them to wearing woolly socks and under-pants.

Guerrilla tactics forced the Romans south until Hadrian stopped the tribes-men with his famous wall. Then, in 142 AD, Antoninus Pius pushed them back and built a turf wall between the Forth and the Clyde, but after twenty years the Antonine Wall was abandoned.

When the Occupation ended in 409 AD, Roman rule had made a lasting impact on Britain. A well organised regime with new towns, good roads and trade with the Empire had encouraged many Britons to adopt the Roman way of life. To north-erners, hot baths and underfloor heating might have been welcome innovations, but there is no sign of these comforts having reached Strathendrick.

Although no evidence has been found, the Balfron area would certainly have been occupied while the Glen-blocker forts were in operation. Balfron's 'Roman Road' is said to have been misnamed, but the same was said in Bearsden until a Roman Bathhouse was discovered. The Balfron road leads to a natural mound which was later fortified by Normans, so the Roman army could also have used this site.

Our only legacy seems to be the hordes of Ballindalloch rabbits for which the Romans must take the blame. Although the Normans are said to have brought them to Britain the trouble began in the 2nd century BC, when the Romans procured these fast breeding mammals from Iberia, which actually means 'the land of rabbits'. Distributing them to be farmed for food may have seemed a good idea till these prolific Spanish exports began to plague the planet.[5]

Darker Days

After the Romans departed from Britain, their Empire slowly collapsed. With the dominant power removed, Scotland became increasingly unstable. Waves of

Roman soldier

invaders moved in while local tribes clashed and harried their neighbours south of the border.

The Scots came from Ireland and fought with the Picts, then the Jutes and Danes followed. Vikings from the Western Isles heaved their longships overland to plunder eastward, taking in Strathendrick on the way. The Angles and Saxons, who were actually German, arrived from England to muscle in. As the Romans had discovered, mountains and rough terrain made the country difficult to annex but isolated communities were easy targets for rape and pillage. As a result of these tribulations the population of Strathendrick probably became an amalgam of the races who invaded their territory.

The Lennox

Strathendrick was in the area which became known as the Lennox. The river Leven flowed from Loch Lomond to the Clyde through a forest of elm trees or 'leamhan' and the word evolved tortuously to give the Lennox its name. The lands of Lennox resembled a minor kingdom ruled by a High Steward, or Mormaor, whose domain included Loch Lomond, East and West Dumbartonshire, and the seven Stirlingshire Parishes of Balfron, Buchanan, Campsie, Drymen, Fintry, Killearn and Strathblane. In 1034 the Lennox and Strathclyde were joined within the kingdom of Duncan I. Later, King William the Lion created the

Earldom of Lennox and bestowed it on his brother Prince David, from whom it passed on to successive Lennox Earls.[6]

The Drummonds

Before 1350 Balfron was held by the Drummonds of Drummond who also owned lands in Roseneath, Auchindown and Cardross in Menteith. According to tradition they were Hungarians who arrived in Scotland during the 11th century with Edgar Atheling and his sister Margaret who married King Malcolm Canmore.[7] The seat of the Drummonds became known as Drymen, which is a corruption of their name. Their clan chief, Malcolm Beg Drummond gifted Cardross to the parsonage of Inchmahome, on the Lake of Menteith in 1220. Eight years later Inchmahome Priory was established on the island and the Drummonds chose that place for their burial ground. Malcolm Beg was Senechal of Lennox and he married the Earl's daughter. In 1363 Margaret, a daughter of Sir Malcolm Drummond of Drummond, was married on Inchmahome to become the second wife of King David II.[8]

According to Drummond records, the patronage and tithes of Balfron church had by then been granted to the Abbey of Inchaffray in 1303 by Sir Malcolm's third son, Thomas Drummond.[9] As the Drummond fortunes increased their lands in Stirlingshire were exchanged for more fertile tracts in Perthshire and in 1605 the

A section of the Bayeux Tapestry

4th Lord Drummond was granted the Earldom of Perth.[10]

Woodend Motte

An early feature in Balfron's history was Woodend Motte, about a mile east of Ballindalloch. Around 1100 the Scottish King David I had difficulty governing his subjects and decided to bring them to heel by delegating authority. Norman knights were invited into Scotland and offered grants of land in return for their administrative skills. The Normans' power to dominate derived largely from their ability to create instant castles known as mottes.

A defensive timber tower with a palisade could be built on a natural eminence or a mound of earth.[11] By commandeering local labour, both mound and motte could be constructed in a few weeks. An adjoining enclosure, known as a bailey would have buildings for stables, workshops and stores and, beyond it, a surrounding ditch or water filled moat would add protection. A stylised motte, depicted in the Bayeux Tapestry, is shown under attack. From the fort on top of the mound, soldiers are hurling spears at the enemy while horsemen charge the entrance bridge which spans the surrounding ditch. Foot soldiers are attacking the wooden palisade of the fort

Norman knight

with firebrands held aloft on spears. Wooden forts were not very durable.

Woodend Motte displayed authority and policed the surrounding area, controlling the routes north and south across the nearby ford, as well as that which followed the Endrick valley to Stirling.[12] There seem to be no records regarding the motte so its history is unknown. The Endrick may have altered course, making travellers use another ford a mile down river, and this could explain why the Norman motte was supplanted by Ballindalloch Castle.

The Clachan, the Kirk and the Castle

The village of Balfron has grown from a few dwellings grouped on a junction of roads. In the days of Woodend Motte the Christian religion was central to community life and an early Kirk of Balfron is

likely to have been established there, on or near the site of our present Parish Church.[13] The feudal system was based on mutual support and a parish church performed an essential roll by upholding the monarchy and uniting vassals with the overlords who gave them protection.[14] The Clachan would have begun as a cluster of tied cottages with occupants bound in service to the lords of Woodend Motte and later, of Ballindalloch Castle. This feudal arrangement eventually led to the development of present day Balfron.

The first record of Ballindalloch in 1238 has already been mentioned, but around 1350 a significant event took place when the lands of Ballindalloch and Kilfasset were granted by charter to Sir Andrew Cunningham and 400 years of Cunningham dominance began.[15]

CHAPTER 4

THE CUNNINGHAM
EARLS OF GLENCAIRN

Ballindalloch was granted to the Earl of Wigtown rewarding his loyalty to the Bruces and from him the land was passed to the Cunninghams.

The Earldom of Wigtown

Robert Fleming was one of Robert the Bruce's right hand men. He was at Dumfries in 1305 when Bruce entered the church and murdered Sir John Comyn, the Red Comyn, who was his rival for the throne. Fleming assisted Bruce in despatching the victim and cut off his head for good measure. Displaying the gory trophy he cried 'Let the deid shaw' which became the Fleming motto. His loyalty was rewarded with lands which had belonged to the late Comyn.

When Bruce died in 1329 his son, David II, succeeded him at the tender age of five, already married to Joanna, daughter of Edward II of England. Four years later the Scottish army was defeated by Balliol and Fleming's son Malcolm

provided refuge for the young King and Queen in Dumbarton Castle. He then helped them escape to France. Malcolm's wife Marjorie had been the King's nurse. When the monarchy was restored in 1341, the King rewarded Malcolm with the Earldom of Wigtown and granted him lands in Lennox. The Earl then passed Ballindalloch to the Cunninghams.

The Cunninghams of Kilmaurs

The founder of the Cunningham dynasty was Wernebald, a Norman who came to Scotland about 1140 in the train of Hugh de Morville and was granted Kilmaurs in North Ayrshire.[1] His family took the name of the district which is still known as Cunningham. 'Cunning' or 'coney' is an old name for a rabbit so a vicious looking pair have been adopted as supporters on the Cunningham coat-of-arms. Meanwhile the conies continue to breed in Ayrshire and at Ballindalloch.

In 1296 Robert Cunningham of Kilmaurs swore fealty to Edward I, but ten

14th-century dress code for the Earl and Countess

years later he changed his allegiance to Robert the Bruce.[2] When King Robert was securely on the throne, Cunningham's loyalty was rewarded and thereafter, he and his successors flourished.

Over Fork Over

The Cunningham shield displays a heraldic 'device' which looks like the letter 'Y'. It is a 'shakefork', a primitive pitchfork made from the branch of a tree. The motto is 'Over Fork Over'.

After King Duncan I was murdered by Macbeth, his son Malcolm, heir to the Scottish throne, had to flee for his life. According to tradition, he was hotly pursued by Macbeth's troops when he came to friendly territory where Cunning-

hams were hay-making. Malcolm leapt into a half made stack yelling 'Over fork over' and was quickly enveloped in hay. By the time Macbeth's men arrived their quarry was safely hidden in a field full of haystacks. The fugitive survived to vanquish Macbeth and be crowned King Malcolm III, known as Canmore.

The Earldom of Glencairn

The Cunninghams acquired land and power through backing the right side and making advantageous marriages. The second Sir William Cunningham of Kilmaurs gained Glencairn in Dumfriesshire and Finlaystone in Renfrewshire through marrying the heiress Margaret Danielston, but his ambitions did not stop there because, after she died, he was granted papal dispensation to marry Lady Mary Stewart, daughter of King Robert III.[3] It would have been a brilliant match but there is no record of a marriage having taken place. Nevertheless, the lady did form a connection with Ballindalloch which is recorded in the next chapter. The Cunninghams became one of the most powerful families in Scotland when, in 1488 William's grandson, Alexander was rewarded for loyal services to King James III by being elevated by royal charter to the dignity of Earl of Glencairn.[4]

The Life of a Medieval Earl

The King of Scots had the absolute right to charter land to his earls as he saw fit. On the accession of a king and on the succes-

24

sion of an earl new charters were granted. If an earl failed to accord loyalty to the crown his earldom could be forfeited causing his livelihood to be lost. An earl had the right to parcel out his lands to his adherents or members of his family and they in turn had the same rights over those who served them.

To govern castles and estates which were often far flung, an earl had to travel

Armorial bearings of the Earls of Glencairn

THE BALLINDALLOCH TREE

AD

1200 · 1300 · 1400 · 1500

AD · 1200 · 1300 · 1400 · 1500

The Earls of Lennox
were the first feudal superiors of Ballindalloch
(succeeding feudal superiors shown in **bold**)

Drummonds of Drummond

Duncan of Luss

Sir Andrew Cunningham c.1350 was granted a charter of
Ballindalloch by **Malcolm Fleming 1st Earl of Wigtown**

Sir Humphrey Cunningham of Glengarnock
m. Jean dau. of Walter Buchanan of Buchanan

William Cunningham of Glengarnock
resigned Ballindalloch to his grandson in 1463

Son

Sir Umfrid Cunygam of Glengernok [sic]
m. Elizabeth dau. of Sir William Edmonstone of Duntreath
and Lady Mary Stewart dau. of King Robert III

John Cunningham of Glengarnock
resigned Ballindalloch to his grandson in 1599

Wernebald c.1140

Robert son of Wernebald c.1160

Robert son of Robert, son of Wernebald c.1180

Richard de Cunningham c.1220

Hervey de Cunningham of Kilmaurs fought at Battle of Largs 1263

Edward de Cunningham of Kilmaurs c.1299
m. Mary dau. Great Steward of Scotland

Reginald Cunningham
m. Janet Riddel heiress of Glengarnock

Robert de Cunningham of Kilmaurs
c.1306

Sir Gilbert Cunningham of Glengarnock
c.1300

Hugh de Cunningham of Kilmaurs
c.1328

Sir William Cunningham of Kilmaurs c.1350

Sir William Cunningham of Kilmaurs m. Margaret
heiress to Glencairn dau. of Sir Robert Danielston of that ilk

Sir Robert Cunningham of Kilmaurs d. before 1450
m. Anne dau. of Sir John de Montgomery of Ardrossan

Alexander 1st Earl of Glencairn d.1488
m. Margaret dau. of Adam Hepburn Lord of Hailes

Robert Cunningham Lord of Kilmaurs
(deprived of Earldom) d. before 1492
m. Christian dau. of Lord Lindsay of Byres

Cuthbert 3rd Earl of Glencairn
d. 1540 m. Marion dau. of Earl of Angus

William 4th Earl of Glencairn d.1547
m. 1. Catherine dau. of Lord Borthwick
2. Elizabeth heiress of John Campbell of West Loudon

Alexander 5th Earl of Glencairn d.1574
m. 1. Janet dau. of Earl of Arran
2. Janet dau. of Sir John Cunningham of Caprington

William 6th Earl of Glencairn d. before 1580
m. Janet dau. of Sir John Gordon of Lochinvar

1600 — 1700 — 1800 — 1900 — 2000

William Cunningham
m. Isobel Scott, predeceased his father

Catherine m. 1612 Sir James Cunningham of Glengarnock
1st Baron of Ballindalloch, resigned Ballindalloch 1613

John Cunningham of Drumbeg WS
granted a charter of Ballindalloch 1687

William Cunningham of Drumbeg & Ballindalloch
m. Martha dau. of Sir George Suttie Bart.

George Cunningham of Drumbeg & Ballindalloch
m. Esther Jolly, escaped assassination 1750

William Cunningham of Ballindalloch, sold out 1786

Robert Dunmore of Ballindalloch 1744-99
m. Janet dau. of John Napier of Ballikinrain, bought estate 1786

Samuel Cooper of Ballindalloch 1765-1842
bought estate 1800 m. Janet heiress of Henry Ritchie

Henry Cooper of Ballindalloch 1816-82
m. Mary Butler

William Cooper of Ballindalloch 1856-1920
m. Matilda Clarke, estate sold by heirs 1923

Norman Donaldson of Ballindalloch 1878-1955
m. Catherine dau. of John Fraser of Balfunning

John Glen 1924-
m. Jill Donaldson, bought house in 1957

Alexander Stephen of Ballindalloch 1927-
m. Susan Thomson, bought property in 1976

John 11th Earl of Glencairn d. 1703
m. 1 Jean dau. of Earl of Mar
2. Margaret heiress of Napier of Kilmahew

Margaret
m. Nicol Graham of Gartmore

Robert Cunninghame-Graham
of Gartmore

Henry Cooper of Ballindalloch
1852-1907
m. Jessie Westcott

James 7th Earl of Glencairn d.1631
m. 1 dau. of Colin Campbell of Glenurquhy
2. Agnes dau. of Sir James Hay of Kingask

William 8th Earl of Glencairn d. before 1635
m. Janet dau. of Earl of Lothian

William 9th Earl of Glencairn c.1610-64
m. 1 Anne dau. of Earl of Findlater
2. Margaret dau. of Earl of Eglinton

Alexander 10th Earl d.1670
m. Nicholas [sic] dau. of Sir James Stewart of Kirkhill

William 12th Earl of Glencairn d. 1734
m. Henrietta dau. of Earl of Galloway

William 13th Earl of Glencairn d. 1755
m. Elizabeth co-heiress of Hugh McGuire of Drumdow

James 14th Earl 1749-91

John 15th Earl of Glencairn
1750-96 m. Isabella dau. of
Earl of Buchan

with his retinue. From time to time the Earl of Glencairn would arrive at Ballindalloch accompanied by fifty men or more, with armed knights and a train of pack animals conveying his furniture and domestic utensils, as well as his hawks and hounds. While in residence, he would travel to Stirling to attend the king and deal locally with matters concerning the Ballindalloch lands. Sport, society and entertainment would also be enjoyed.

Being lavishly attended, the Earl and his Lady would occupy the Great Chamber for several weeks while the rest took their bed rolls and dossed down where they could, which was mostly on the rush strewn floor in the Great Hall. In crowded quarters without drains, the dirt and stench would gradually become unendurable. Provisions were supplied from rents paid in kind, but after a time the stores would run out so that the company would be glad to move on and allow the resident staff to clean up and restock. As an earl's 'perambulations' could be almost continuous, few records of these visits have survived.

The Earldom Forfeited

Alexander's glory as an Earl was short lived because within months he was killed at the Battle of Sauchieburn when the king he had loyally supported met with defeat and also lost his life. The successful usurper, James IV, took a dim view of the House of Glencairn for not having backed him and withheld the Earldom from Alexander's heir. This act of revenge has caused confusion among historians because some do not now recognise Robert Cunningham as the 2nd Earl of Glencairn. This publication prefers to allow him the benefit of the doubt.

Restoration and Divided Loyalties

The demoted Earl was never reinstated, but James IV finally accepted Robert's son Cuthbert as 3rd Earl of Glencairn. William the 4th Earl prospered and extended the Earldom into nine Scottish counties but disaster fell when he was taken prisoner by the English at the rout of Solway Moss.[5] William used his wits and got himself ransomed for £1,000 by promoting the 'Rough Wooing' of Henry VIII, who sought to arrange a marriage between the young Queen of Scots and his son Prince Edward. Though hardly patriotic, the Earl even supported the English king as Protector of Scotland but Glenciarn was eventually granted remission.[6]

The Good Earl and John Knox

Alexander, the 5th Earl was one whose sojourn at Ballindalloch was actually recorded.[7] He was called 'The Good Earl' which suggests that he was not as bad as some of the others though his first wife Janet might not have agreed. She bore him four children before he divorced her – no doubt taking his lead from Henry VIII. Next time round Alexander strengthened his Cunningham links by marrying another Janet, the daughter of his kinsman

Alexander, 5th Earl of Glencairn
(courtesy of the National Galleries of Scotland)

defeat her at the Battle of Langside.

In 1556 Glencairn displayed his religious ardour by inviting John Knox to celebrate Communion in his garden at Finlaystone. When the Earl's family and friends were assembled the proceedings were disrupted through a serious omission. There were no Communion cups. The Glencairn household was further disconcerted when Knox declared that consecrated wine should not be offered from a drinking vessel which had been used for frivolous purposes. In the end some candlesticks were produced and the problem was solved by turning them upside down so that celebrants could drink the wine from their hollow bases.

Sir John Cunningham of Caprington near Kilmaurs.

Earl Alexander hedged his bets. He supported the Reformation and gained a fat pension for upholding Henry VIII as Protector of Scotland though, after the murder of Rizzio, he sided with Mary Queen of Scots at the battle of Dunbar. When she was captured and imprisoned on Loch Leven he turned against her.[8] In a fit of Protestant zeal, he and his accomplices wrecked her royal chapel at Holyrood and tore down the altar. He then assisted the downfall of his Catholic Queen by commanding a division to

16th century dress code for the Earl and Countess

29

John Knox
(courtesy of the National Galleries of Scotland)

For many years these unusual Communion cups continued to be used in the local church.[9]

The Ruthven Raiders

When the Scottish Queen went into exile her son James VI was still a child, so Scotland was ruled by a succession of Regents. During this period of instability the 7th Earl of Glencairn was one of the Ruthven Raiders who conspired against the teenage King because they suspected him of becoming a Catholic like his mother. In 1582 the Earl of Gowrie led the insurrection which kidnapped King James and held him prisoner in Ruthven Castle. After the young monarch managed to escape, Gowrie was duly tried for treason and publicly beheaded. Glencairn met with better luck. He managed to keep his head and even retained his seat on the Privy Council.[10]

Civil War and the Glencairn Rising

William the 9th Earl who liked to operate on a grand scale was a loyal supporter of Charles I. In the 1640s he was not only appointed a Privy Councillor, but also Commissioner of the Treasury and Lord Justice General. When Civil War broke out he declared for the King which meant that the inhabitants of Balfron would have been required to support the Royalist cause regardless of their personal loyalties.

In a country oppressed under Cromwell's Commonwealth, the Earl of Glencairn served as Governor of His Majesty's Forces in the Highlands of Scotland. His military manoeuvres met with varying results. In Menteith a successful engagement took place in 1653 when he raised nearly three hundred Highlanders to repel a detachment of Roundheads from Stirling Castle. The Highland cavalry and infantry assembled at Duchray Castle and proceeded to ambush the advancing troops in the pass of Aberfoyle. Substantial losses drove the enemy to retreat while clansmen clambered among the crags and harried their assailants from the high ground.

The following year Glencairn marshalled an army and marched north to oppose General Monck, who commanded Cromwell's army in Scotland. On the way, the Earl encouraged recruits by distributing Presbyterian leaflets, but the Highlanders were more enthused when his colleague, Lord Kenmure, lured them with a barrel of whisky. On reaching Dornoch, Glencairn threw a party to celebrate the handing over of his troops to General Middleton but discord soon broke out when he began boasting about the military prowess of his men. Sir George Munro declared them to be 'no other than a pack of thieves and robbers'. Glencairn was incensed and challenged him to a duel with pistols – on horseback. When both of them missed they dismounted and resumed the dispute at ground level.[11] Hostilities ended when Sir George retired with a cut eyebrow, but Glencairn was not appeased.

The disgruntled Earl stormed south again, accompanied by his men. A defeat at Dunkeld did nothing to cool his wrath and finding Dumbarton Castle in enemy hands, he vented his fury by mounting an attack. Despite despatching thirty Roundheads Glencairn's triumph was short lived because he was taken prisoner and carted off to await execution in Edinburgh

William, 9th Earl of Glencairn
(courtesy of the National Galleries of Scotland)

Castle. Just before he met his doom, the monarchy was restored and Charles II appointed him Lord High Chancellor of Scotland.[12]

With his fortunes restored more indignities beset him. King Charles required his earls to be Episcopalians but Glencairn's Presbyterian spirit could not comply. When Bishop Sharp assumed precedence over him the Earl sank into a decline. But before his final collapse he managed to do his bit for Balfron by installing a badly needed minister in the much neglected Kirk. He then retired to his death bed with a clear conscience and his demise was duly attended by Presbyterian ministers. True to form, Glencairn departed in style and was ceremoniously consigned to his tomb at St Giles where 'aught trumpetoires sounding at the grave's mouth ended the solempnitie'.[13]

The Eglinton Feud

The Cunninghams had always been a fractious family and for centuries they carried on a feud with the Montgomeries of Eglinton Castle which was barely five miles from Kilmaurs. Trouble came to a head in 1448 when James II unwisely granted Sir Alexander Montgomerie of Eglinton, and his heirs, the office of Bailie of the Barony of Cunningham, which had until then been held by the Cunninghams.[14] The furious Cunninghams burned down Eglinton Castle and the Earl of Eglinton retaliated by occupying the steeple at Kilmaurs with a hundred Montgomerie men.[15]

The vendetta continued. In 1586 a band of Cunninghams assassinated 'the fattest of the Montgomeries', namely Hugh, 4th Earl of Eglinton.[16] In reprisal for his part in the crime Patrick Cunningham 'was shot near his ain hoose at Aiket'.

For years the Privy Council was disrupted by the quarrelling Earls and, during the 'Red Parliament of Perth' in 1606, an unruly battle broke out between their warring attendants. The antagonists fought through the long summer evening 'fra seven till ten hours with great skaith'

The Eglinton Feud

but, on that occasion, only one Cunningham bit the dust.[17]

Bitter feelings between the rival houses were finally resolved when the 9th Earl suppressed his quarrelsome nature and married Margaret Montgomerie, daughter of the 6th Earl of Eglinton.

The Struggling Succession

John, 11th Earl of Glencairn was a military man who raised a regiment to support the Revolution of William III. Like his predecessors he became a Privy Councillor and Governor of Dumbarton Castle. Though married twice there was only one son to succeed him so the dynasty seemed rather shaky till William, his heir, became the 12th Earl and improved the outlook by producing eight sons. The 13th Earl, another William, served in the army and achieved the rank of Major General. He sold Kilmaurs and transferred the Glencairn seat to Finlaystone where a mansion was built to replace the old castle. Again the succession seemed assured when he fathered four sons even though the youngest died in childhood and the eldest predeceased him while serving king and country.

Robert Burns

The second son James became the 14th Earl. He too followed a military career but never married. Instead he enjoyed the bachelor life and became a patron of Robert Burns. When the farmer poet had been suffering a period of 'wretchedness

and exile' an invitation to Finlaystone cheered him greatly. The introduction had been made by the Earl's factor, as the Burns country in Ayrshire was largely owned by Glencairn. In playful mood, the bard celebrated his visit by scratching his signature on one of the window panes using a diamond ring and cheekily added the date of the bottle which he and the Earl were drinking. There was merry roistering with music, poetry and song. The Earl even arranged his employment as an exciseman so Rabbie regarded Glencairn as his 'one true patron' but in 1791 the Earl died suddenly from pneumonia and his influential backing came to an abrupt end.[18]

The Earldom passed to the third son, John, who did not share his brother's passion for poetry so Rabbie found himself bereft and penned a mournful lament which ended:

The mother may forget the child
That smiles sae sweetly on her knee
But I'll remember thee Glencairn
And a' that thou hast done for me!

The Fall of the House of Glencairn

John, the 15th Earl, departed from Glencairn tradition when he abandoned the army and took holy orders in the Church of England. Five years after succeeding he died without issue in 1796 and there was no one to follow him. The Fergussons of Kilkerran and several other branches of the Cunningham family laid claim to the Earldom, but none were successful and the title became extinct.[19]

When the last Earl died, Finlaystone was entailed to Robert Graham of Gartmore. His mother was formerly Lady Margaret Cunningham, eldest daughter of the 11th Earl and thereafter, the Gartmore family took the name of Cunninghame Graham. A notable descendant was the eccentric 'Don Roberto' Cunninghame Graham who was in his time a gaucho in South America, a writer, a poet, a Member of Parliament supporting the Labour movement and finally the first president of the Scottish National Party. Another distinguished member of that family was Admiral Sir Angus Cunninghame Graham of Ardoch. The family no longer owns Gartmore but their graves can still be seen in the beautiful ruins of Inchmaholm Priory on the Lake of Menteith.

At Caprington Castle, Robert Cunninghame keeps the shakefork banner flying and it is claimed that the 'Over Fork Over' adventure took place on his land. His wife uses the motto as her e-mail address, which is doubly appropriate as Rosie Cunninghame is a Garden Designer.

CHAPTER 5

THE CUNNINGHAMS
OF BALLINDALLOCH

While the Earls of Glencairn came and went from Ballindalloch over four centuries, their Cunningham kinsmen were required to hold the fort and manage the land.

Sir Andrew Cunningham

During the troubled reign of King David II Ballindalloch was held by Duncan of Luss.[1] Then, about 1350 the Earl of Wigtown granted a charter of Kilfasset and Ballindalloch in Lennox to Sir Andrew Cunningham, a younger son of Hugh de Cunningham of Kilmaurs.[2] Andrew was then appointed constable of the castle, to take charge of the property and perform the duties of tenant-in-chief, an hereditary office.

Succession to the lairdship depended on the superior granting a charter, in the same way that he was beholden to the King. The Cunningham lairds of Ballindalloch appear to have maintained a good relationship with their superiors as the property passed down their family for many generations. It is unclear exactly how and when the feudal superiority was transferred from the Earldom of Lennox, through Drummond and Wigtown, but it appears that thereafter the superior of Ballindalloch was Cunningham of Kilmaurs.

Glengarnock

When Sir Andrew died in 1388, his son and heir was described as 'Sir Humphrey Cunningham of Glengarnock'. The Cunninghams had acquired that property when Reginald, a younger son of Edward Cunningham of Kilmaurs, married Janet Riddel, heiress of Glengarnock. When Reginald's son died without an heir the title passed to the Ballindalloch branch of the family who became Cunninghams of Glengarnock, taking the name of the senior property.[3]

In the Cunninghame district of Ayrshire the awesome remains of Glengarnock Castle can still be seen where the River Garnock carves its way through a

Above. Glengarnock Castle (Pont and Dobbie).

Left. Plan of Glengarnock Castle (McGibbon and Ross)

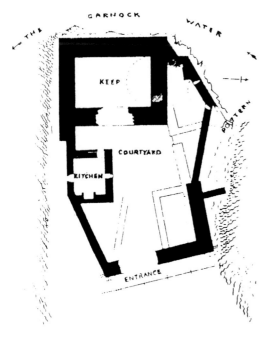

wild expanse of moorland. On three sides there is an eighty foot drop to the river and, on the fourth, a narrow causeway once gave access to what must have been an almost impregnable castle.[4] While secure from attack, it would have been grim being holed up on that remote, windswept moor. By 1775 the castle was in ruins as the Cunninghams of Glengarnock had abandoned it, preferring Ballindalloch and the gentler countryside of Strathendrick.

Sir Umfrid and the Merry Widow

When Humphrey's great-grandson succeeded him the Cunningham fortunes were flying high because 'Sir Umfrid Cunygam of Glengernok' outstripped his ambitious kinsmen by wedding a royal bride. Elizabeth Edmonstone was almost 'the girl next door' as her home was at Duntreath less than five miles away. Her parents were Sir William Edmonstone and Lady Mary Stewart, daughter of King Robert III.[5]

Being a royal princess had made Elizabeth's mother immensely desirable and, due to recurring widowhood, she had been claimed by no less than four husbands in succession. One by one she had wedded George Douglas Earl of Angus, James Kennedy younger of Dunure, Sir William Graham of Kincardine and Sir William Edmonstone of Culloden.[6] The popular princess played her part by producing offspring for all of them. Umfrid's kinsman, Sir William Cunningham of Kilmaurs had also pressed his suit and had even been granted papal dispensation, because his late wife and his intended bride were closely related. But after the pope had sanctioned the proposed union it seems that Cunningham was side lined. Edmonstone won the lady's hand and, due to his prestigious marriage in 1425, he was granted the Barony and lands of Duntreath.[7]

Sir William and Lady Mary made their home at Duntreath Castle and, having raised their family there, they were well placed to enjoy their grand-children along at Ballindalloch. When Lady Mary died she was buried in the Parish Kirk of Strathblane. Many years later, in 1844 Sir Archibald Edmonstone, 3rd Baronet, ordered the tomb to be reopened to make certain she was inside, and sure enough, she was. While her royal remains were being disinterred a tooth fell out and Edmon-stone retained it as 'an interesting family relic'.[8] The present Sir Archie disclaims all knowledge of the celebrated souvenir, but maybe a guest at the castle will one day discover Lady Mary's missing tooth at the back of a bedroom drawer.

15th-century dress code for Sir Umfrid and Lady Elizabeth Cunningham

The Barony of Ballindalloch

John Cunningham of Glengarnock was the next laird on record. He was predeceased by his son, so in 1599 he 'resigned' Ballindalloch to his grandson Sir James Cunningham who was that year granted a Charter by King James VI 'erecting' the lands into the Free Barony of Ballindalloch, with the Castle of Ballindalloch ordained to be the principal messuage. In 1612 Sir James strengthened the bond with his feudal superior by marrying Lady Catherine Cunningham, daughter of the 7th Earl of Glencairn.[9]

James and Catherine did not enjoy Ballindalloch for long. In 1613 the Barony was resigned due to what seems to have been a mortgage involving the Cunninghams of Drumquhassle and their cadets the Cunninghams of Drumbeg, while Buchanan of Buchanan was also involved in the transactions.[10] At a time of unrest which led to the Civil War, Drumquhassle fell on hard times and much of the land there was sold. During this period the ownership of Ballindalloch is unclear, but after 1648 the estate passed to the Cunninghams of Drumbeg and in 1687 John Cunningham of Drumbeg was granted the Barony of Ballindalloch. He was a Writer to the Signet and thus a new species of landowner. The Barony cannot have yielded sufficient income for him to live comfortably without an additional livelihood. Subsequently, his grandson, George, was required to administer baronial justice when Balfron was suddenly pitched into the limelight.

The Abduction of Jean Key

In 1750 a scandalous crime took place within the Barony of Ballindalloch. The incident occurred at Edinbellie, half a mile east of Balfron. A teenage widow known by her maiden name as Jean Key (or Kay) was staying there, at her parental home, two months after the untimely death of her husband, John Wright of Easter Glins. Wright was said to have been a rich man so Jean had inherited his fortune. Robin Oig MacGregor, the youngest son of the outlawed Rob Roy, wanted the money badly and set out to marry the widow. So,

17th-century dress code for the Baron and his Lady

The Abduction Jean Key at Edinbellie

on a dark December evening, he rode to Edinbellie with two of his brothers and a fearsome band of clansmen, all heavily armed with broadswords, pistols and dirks. Robin had already tried to force his attentions on Jean, so when he turned up with his ruffian gang she locked herself in a closet. While her family tried in vain to protect her, the intruders forced their way in and dragged Jean off, still 'fcreiching and crying'. Without shoes or even a cloak she was flung across a horse while they rode through the night to Rowardennan. A dubious minister was summoned from

Glasgow and a marriage took place in spite of her protests.[11] Afterwards, Robin claimed Jean had gone with him willingly and the abduction had been faked to overcome her mother's objections to their marriage. George Cunningham, the Baron of Ballindalloch, played his part by issuing a warrant for the arrest of Robin Oig and his two conspiring brothers.

There were many attempts to rescue Jean and bring her captors to justice while they dragged her about the highlands dodging officers of the law. Eventually she was freed but never recovered from her ordeal and within a year she died from smallpox. Three years after the abduction Robin was finally brought to trial and both he and the minister who performed the forced marriage were hanged. Reports tell that Robin confronted the gallows in a manner both courtly and contrite, and afterwards his body was grandly conveyed to join his highland ancestors. Jean already lay buried in the old churchyard of Kippen not far from Wright Park, a fine mansion which was being built at the time of her abduction and might have become her marital home.[12]

Later a gang of MacGregors set out to avenge Robin Oig, the target being George Cunningham who had issued the arrest warrant. They staged an ambush at the Clachan of Balfron and lay in wait by the old oak tree which stands there to this day. Being conveniently close to the pub, the gunmen may have over imbibed because the would-be assassins shot the wrong man. Buchanan of Cremanan, who was passing by, fell victim to the crime and the lucky Baron survived.[13]

When outlaws and villains become sufficiently notorious, they always seem to get a good press. Sir Walter Scott wove a romantic aura around Rob Roy and the crimes which he committed, while Robert Louis Stevenson portrayed the lawless Robin Oig as hardly less than a perfect gentleman.[14]

The End of an Era

George's son Colonel William Cunningham of the 58th Regiment of Foot ended a 436 year dynasty of tenure when he sold Ballindalloch on the 11th October 1786. The last Earl of Glencairn died ten years later. The sale price was £8,500 but by then the Barony lands were probably a fraction of what the Cunninghams had once owned.

Sadly, the Cunningham era seems to have left no lasting mark on the Parish of Balfron. When Stirling was the capital of Scotland and the Earls of Glencairn were attending Court and holding high office for the Crown, Ballindalloch was a place of considerable importance. Now that their castle no longer exists, four centuries of Cunningham dominion might never have taken place. Despite their long and eventful history Balfron has nothing which bears the name of Cunningham or of Glencairn. Only their story remains.

But all is not lost. Some hardy rhododendrons which flourish on the Ballindalloch avenue just happen to be the irrepressible 'Cunningham's White' and more reticent 'Cunningham's Blush'.

CHAPTER 6

BARONS AND BARONIES

A Scottish Barony was normally granted by the King giving a Charter directly to a Baron who became his Tenant-in-chief.[1] Although the early charters were written in Latin, Anglo-Saxon words were included giving the Baron the rights of 'soke and sake', 'toll and team', and 'infangdthief' (but not outfangdthief !) all of which defied translation into Latin. It is suggested that even when the Charters were granted the meanings of these words had already been lost and nobody knew exactly what they meant, but they were included as a matter of form.[2] A Baron's title was hereditary but he could be deposed in which case the title reverted to the King who could then reissue it. A Baron was required to administer the King's justice and held court at his 'caput', normally his castle, although some Charters stipulated that the court was to be held at a specific place in the open air. Baronies thus became units of local justice. A County Sheriff, also responsible to the King, supervised Barons to ensure that justice was fairly dispensed. A Baron would normally chair his court although he could delegate the responsibility to his Baillie.

He had the right of 'fossa et furca',

herself, the practice was discontinued. The crime of treason could not be tried by a Baron as that was a matter for the King.

A Baron was required to provide men for military service and ensure that his tenants practised their archery. He controlled the smithy and owned the brewery and the mill, charging what he pleased for their products. Millers tended to be unpopular because they were the lairds' men and notorious for overcharging.

Some Baronies were totally responsible to the king but Ballindalloch was part of the Earldom of Glencairn and the Baron had to obey his Earl as well as the King. How the demarcation operated is not clear but the system appears to have worked for many centuries.

The first charter for the Barony of Ballindalloch, granted and signed by James VI in 1599, was to James Cunningham of Glengarnock.[3] It included the lands of Polgaris (Balgair), Kilfassitis (Kilfasset), Keirhill and Ballindalloch with its castle, wards, tenants etc. It referred to the millstone quarry of Polgairs, the mill of Kilfassitis and the right to 'win' peats in the moss of Cremanan. Each of the properties mentioned would have been occupied by a bonnet laird and included several farms. The Charter, written in Latin, specified that the 'principal messuage' was to be Ballindalloch Castle.

The size and importance of Baronies

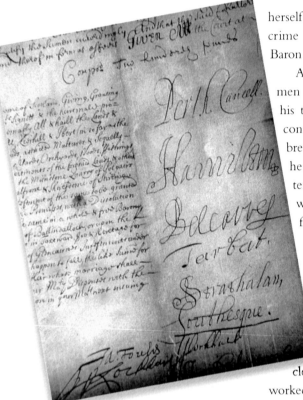

Extract from the Ballindalloch Charter of 1599

meaning pit and gallows, which gave him power to hang a man: drowning in a water filled pit was considered a more ladylike form of capital punishment for a female miscreant. Pit and gallows were rarely used and a Baron dealt mostly with matters such as debt, theft, land disputes, broken fences and personal feuds. Public punishment was used as a deterrent. At the Clachan of Balfron the oak tree was fitted with chains and iron collars, known as 'jougs', which were used to detain offenders. However, after a woman strangled

varied. The Barony of Ballindalloch, covered the Parish of Balfron and at times included land south of the Endrick such as Parkhall, Carbeth and Croy Cunningham as well as Uchtermachny and Kildynny in Perthshire.[4]

One Charter stipulated that 'miln-stones' which were quarried and shaped at Balgair should not damage crops when they were put on edge and rolled the two miles to the mill at Kilfasset. The Baron of Ballindalloch was obliged to keep the local wolf population under control, paying two shillings to anyone who killed a wolf whelp. Had he held office in the Dark Ages, Balfron's lupine disaster, might have been averted. An unscrupulous Baron

'Noose at ten'

could abuse the trust placed in him. This must have happened quite often as even now the pantomime villain is frequently 'The bold, bad Baron' although he may soon be usurped by the 'bold, bad Banker'.

William Nimmo, in his History of Stirlingshire 1777, did not have a high opinion of the local barons and said 'the landlords were diftinguifhed by a ruftic fort of hofpitality, and often carried their entertainments to the higheft degree of intemperance . . .'. Few had enough income to improve their estates and there was no incentive for their tenants to do so either. The owner of an estate might try to upgrade his property but the next genera-tion would allow it to go downhill 'and fpend the wealth acquired by the induftry of his parents in diffipation and riotous idlenefs'. These criticisms may have applied to the Cunningham Barons of Ballindalloch as there is no record of their having done much that was constructive apart from marrying well connected ladies. The 'low ftate of agriculture' in the Parish and the fact that Balfron Kirk was always having financial troubles could have been an indication of Cunningham 'idlenefs'.

As communications improved there was less need for Barons' courts and in 1747 they were abolished. However Baronies still exist and are recorded in Title Deeds and in the Land Register. The powers of the Baron have been eroded and now it would be politically incorrect

43

Armorial bearings of Alexander Stephen of Linthouse Baron of Ballindalloch taken from the Letters Patent by the Herald Painter at the Court of the Lord Lyon.

Ballindalloch', because his great grand-father took the name of the family ship-yard at Linthouse when he registered his coat-of-arms. Today a coat-of-arms may be granted by the Lord Lyon King-of-Arms provided the application is neither improper nor frivolous.

When Ballindalloch Estate changed hands in 1923, the solicitors failed to convey the Barony with the result that it was left in limbo. This piece of Ballindalloch's history was not greatly valued at that time. Sandy Stephen reckoned that reclaiming the barony would make a good retirement hobby, and many years later John Spens, solicitor and Rothesay Herald, gave valuable advice. John Donaldson, who owned the surrounding land, encouraged Sandy in his claim and later John's widow, Charlotte gave vital help concerning the feudal superiority. To ensure that nobody else had a just claim to the barony, searches had to be undertaken, Counsel's Opinions sought and the Registrar of the Land Register satisfied. Finally, after much machination which greatly enriched the legal profession, the Lord Lyon agreed that the title was good. The object had been to preserve the Barony of Ballindalloch for future owners and this is being arranged. Meantime the present Baron of Ballindalloch is delighted

to enforce punitive judgement even if 'He's got a little list'.

Barons and Gentlemen with regis-tered coats-of-arms are described 'of' the place where they were registered. The present Baron could still call himself 'Alexander Stephen of Linthouse Baron of

to offer a reward of two shillings (10p) for any wolf whelp and takes great pride in Balfron being a Wolf Free Zone.

CHAPTER 7

ROBERT DUNMORE

Born in 1744, Robert Dunmore was the son of a successful Glasgow merchant, a wealthy Tobacco Lord who came to be described as 'one of the old Virginia Dons'. Thomas Dunmore was the owner of Kelvinside, which was then a rural estate on the edge of Glasgow. Having made his fortune overseas he used it to make improvements at home. He built a new mansion house at Kelvinside in 1750 and 'originated the ornamental woods which add so much to the picturesque

Kelvinside House

Robert Dunmore 1744–99
(courtesy of the National Galleries of Scotland)

character of the locality'.[1] In 1771 he bought the nearby lands of Gilmorehill in the area now occupied by Glasgow University.[2] Gilmorehill was farmed, and later, part of the land was used as a print field for dying and bleaching fabrics made from linen and cotton. His son, Robert would have been in his late twenties and the print field may have been an early venture into the industry which he would later bring to Balfron.

Though Robert was the youngest of Thomas and Helen Dunmore's seven children he fell heir to a major portion of the Dunmore wealth including Kelvinside and Gilmorehill. Like his father, he became a successful businessman and developed wide interests. These included a partnership with John Napier of Ballikinrain, just across the river from Balfron.[3] In 1776 Robert married Napier's only child, Janet who was heiress to his estate. The Napiers had owned Ballikinrain for about four centuries and were held to be cadets of the Earls of Lennox in whose earldom their property lay. John Napier of Merchiston, the 16th century inventor of logarithms, had been one of Janet's kinsmen. He had lived at Gartness and according to some sources was born at Edinbellie in the parish of Balfron.

Dunmore was regarded as an extremely rich man whose properties included Bankeir, Newlands, Blairskaith and Balwill. In 1786 he bought Ballindalloch from Colonel William Cunningham. Being a man of vision Dunmore used his wealth to improve and benefit the neighbourhood of his home in Strathendrick. The little village of Balfron suddenly entered a new era when he set up the Ballindalloch Cotton Mill in 1789 and brought this quiet corner of Stirlingshire into the Industrial Age.[4] The new development brought prosperity to Balfron and the village rapidly expanded as Dunmore brought in weavers and built more than a hundred houses to accommodate the families of his work force. The mill employed nearly 400 people, including men, women and children, and due to its success, local wages were substantially increased and the whole community thrived.

The countryside began to change as Dunmore launched into a programme of

A winter view of Ballindalloch Mill, by Susan Robson (courtesy of Jim and Audrey Bisset)

improvements in agriculture and forestry. Through his inspired generosity public roads and bridges were constructed, including the Ballindalloch Bridge across the Endrick. Workers who crossed to a bleaching field south of the river, preferred to call it the 'Field Bridge'. Although the bleaching venture was abandoned after only ten years, local people still adhere to this obsolete and unworthy name for one of Dunmore's finest contributions to Balfron. Like this handsomely constructed bridge, the estate bridges at Ballindalloch and Keirhill have for two hundred years continued to serve while withstanding traffic twenty times the weight for which they were designed.

It was said 'Dunmore has given life and fpirit to the country which four years ago feemed condemned to perpetual dulnefs' and has made 'fubftantial enclofures on the Eftate of Ballindalloch where in addition to thefe, there have been feveral plantations of wood formed with an equal regard to beauty and utility'.[5] Dunmore was thereafter 'much respected and deservedly esteemed' and his achievements are all the more remarkable because of the short length of time in which they were accomplished.[6] Three years after starting up his successful Ballindalloch Cotton Mill, Robert Dunmore was bankrupt.

This sudden catastrophe was caused by the French Revolution. In the autumn of 1792 France was gripped in a reign of

18th-century dress code for Ballindalloch gentry

Ballindalloch ceased after only seven years.

When her father died in 1784 Janet had inherited Ballikinrain. As her estate was not at risk when her husband became insolvent, she was able to provide a home where they could live in comfort with their family of five sons and three daughters. Janet's ancestral home was a pretty house with a simple Georgian facade on a courtyard flanked by low buildings. A spacious new wing was built to accommodate their family and the work is believed to have been undertaken prior to Robert's financial losses. This house would have been far more appealing than the old truncated castle at Ballindalloch. Sadly 'Robert Dunmore of Ballikinrain' did not live long to enjoy the property Janet had inherited because he died at the age of fifty-five, only six years after the disaster. Then Janet followed him two years later.[7]

As extensive developments had taken place at Ballindalloch, it is likely that Robert and Janet had rented the estate during the decade before the purchase was made. As a serving officer Colonel Cunningham would have spent periods away from home, so letting the property could have been advantageous to both parties, and it was not unusual for a tenant to undertake improvements in the absence of a landlord.

It is evident that Robert Dunmore had been planning ahead for his eldest son, Thomas, and hoped to establish a Dunmore seat for him to inherit at Ballindalloch. Although Dunmore's purchase

terror when the monarchy was overthrown and a Republic declared. Alarmed by insurrection across the Channel, the British Government hastily summoned parliament and called out the militia throughout Britain. The following month the French King Louis XVI was executed by guillotine. British confidence was undermined and the ensuing commercial crisis caused several banks and merchant houses to fail in the spring of 1793. Robert Dunmore was one of the many unfortunate citizens to fall victim. There was no financial limitation so all his properties were sequestered and resold. Dunmore's great philanthropic projects came abruptly to an end when his ownership of did not go through until 1786, Janet's father had been aware of his son-in-law's plan for Thomas, and before he died Napier had made a settlement in which John, the Dunmore's second son, would succeed his mother by inheriting Ballikinrain.[8] On doing so John changed his name to Dunmore Napier, as did his successors at Ballikinrain. When John died a bachelor his younger brother Robert succeeded him and raised his family there.

Meanwhile Robert Dunmore's eldest son Thomas could no longer inherit the estate which his father had planned for him. Young Thomas had spent his childhood roaming the fields and woods and getting to know the farms at Ballindalloch but when the lad was only fourteen his prospect of succeeding to the Dunmore estate was cruelly extinguished. Displaying his father's grit Thomas joined the army and saw active service overseas, achieving the rank of Commissary General. He later bought back Kilfasset which had formed part of Ballindalloch estate and lay just

across the Endrick from Ballikinrain. Thomas had married a widow, Sarah Steel but their only child, a daughter, predeceased him. Kilfasset was left to his nephew, Captain Robert Dunmore Napier of Ballikinrain. Sadly the Captain's only son died unmarried. With no heir to continue the Dunmore Napier dynasty at Ballikinrain, the estate was sold in 1862 to the industrialist, Sir Archibald Orr Ewing. After Ballikinrain Castle was built the house became known as Old Ballikinrain.[9]

Over the years the Ballindalloch Cotton Mill prospered as farmland flourished and plantations matured so that the village of Balfron continued to thrive and develop as never before. The life of Robert Dunmore leaves many questions unanswered and there is scope for an interesting history to be written about this remarkably benevolent and ill-fated man who, in hardly more that a decade, did more for Balfron than anyone has done before or since.[10]

Ballikinrain House before Robert Dunmore's alterations.

CHAPTER 8

THE COOPER FAMILY

In 1800 Ballindalloch was bought by Samuel Cooper, the second son of William Cooper of Smeithston and Failford.[1] The Coopers had a distinguished family history with a landowning, military and church background. Samuel's elder brother had inherited Failford in Ayrshire but his own prospects were good because, in 1795 he married Janet, the daughter and heiress of Henry Ritchie of Craigton and his wife, Esther Crauford of Balshagray and Scotstown, who descended from the House of Craufordland in Ayrshire. As Janet could anticipate a substantial inheritance, she and Samuel set out to find themselves a country estate and became the owners of Ballindalloch. The amount of land that Samuel purchased is uncertain, but in 1872 the property consisted of 627 acres.

Samuel and Janet lived happily in Stirlingshire and raised a family of ten, with two sons and eight daughters. He became a Lieutenant Colonel in the Stirlingshire militia and a Deputy Lieut-enant of the county. When his elder brother Alexander died unmarried in 1829, Samuel inherited Failford so, in due course, his elder son William succeeded to that property.[2] In 1841 the first National Census recorded Samuel Cooper as a seventy year old widower at Ballindalloch, with the house full of his children and grandchildren. He died the following year.

Most of the Cooper girls seem to have married well. Young Janet wed one of her mother's wealthy relations, William Wallace of Cloncaird, but Henry, the younger son, did not fulfil his parent's hopes because he fell in love with Mary Butler, a beautiful Irish girl from County Wexford. Both families fiercely opposed the match because the Coopers were Protestants and the Butlers were Catholics. To make matters worse, one of Mary's uncles was a full blown Cardinal. In 1846, in the face of general disapproval, the young couple eloped and were married in Glasgow. At the ceremony all proprieties were observed and Mary's wedding veil of

Mary Butler, wife of Henry Cooper   *Henry Cooper JP, 1816–82*

fine Limerick lace became an heirloom which was passed down the family to be worn by her grand-daughters before it was finally bequeathed to the Museum of Costume at Kelvingrove Art Gallery in Glasgow.[3] Soon after the runaway marriage all was forgiven. Henry was reinstated and in due course inherited Ballindalloch.

The reformed rebels settled down and raised a family of eight with three sons and five daughters. Henry and Mary were strongly united on the upbringing of their children, and attended church each Sunday alternating Balfron Kirk with a Catholic service. At that time the nearest chapel was probably at Milngavie, which was nine miles distant, so the local Catholics met in an old weaver's shop in Balfron.[4] When a pipe line for Glasgow's

new water supply was being laid nearby, Irish workers brought their families to live in the village and the need for a chapel became urgent. At Mary's request the Coopers helped to establish St Anthony's Chapel in Dunmore Street. The Balfron chapel was built in 1867 by the Glasgow architect David Thomson who had completed major alterations at Duntreath.

Henry Cooper's family grew up in the rambling old house which had evolved over a century earlier from the former Ballindalloch Castle. The building had been constructed from the porous local red sandstone, probably quarried at Tombrake to the north of Balfron. Having begun as a fortified tower with vaulted ceilings, spiral turnpike stairs and echoing stone floors, it would have been damp, cramped and awkward to staff with a

Ballindalloch House built for Henry Cooper in 1868 (courtesy of RCAHMS)

family of eight lively children rushing about. The Coopers were said to have been a good looking family but, when the time came to launch their daughters into society, Henry and Mary realised their quaint old house did not compare favourably with the gracious dwellings of their neighbours.

In the West of Scotland, industrial wealth and the coming of the railways was creating a demand for country houses with impressive exteriors and spacious rooms for receiving guests, so castles were taking on a new look. In Ayrshire, Henry's kinsmen at Cloncaird had given their castle a massive make-over. At Lennox-town, in 1841 John Lennox-Kincaid saw the completion of a colossal new edifice which he called Lennox Castle, though his claim to the Earldom had not met with

success. His princely palace was followed by a new Buchanan Castle, completed in 1854 for the Duke of Montrose. At nearby Blanefield, the rebuilding of Duntreath Castle was completed for Sir Archibald Edmonstone in 1863. When the Coopers could look out of their windows and observe the turrets of Sir Archibald Orr-Ewing's brand new Ballikinrain Castle steadily rising across the Endrick, Henry decided to act.

David Thomson, the architect, was called in again. Though many Victorians enlarged their houses the Coopers preferred to scrap theirs and follow the Orr-Ewing's example by choosing a new site. The condition of the old building may have influenced them, combined with the appeal of a more attractive location only sixty yards away. While the ancient

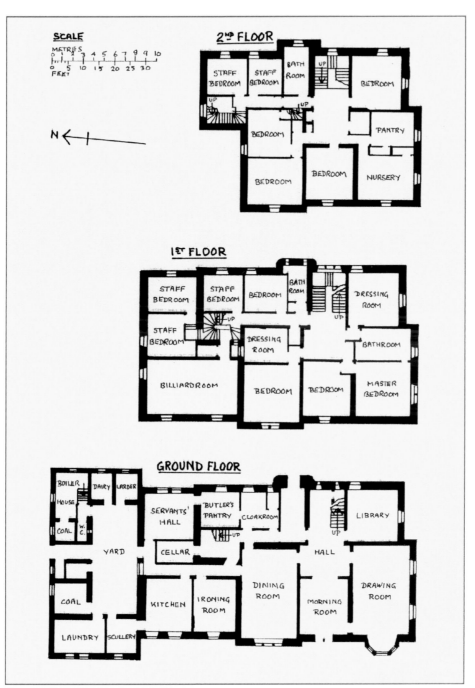

Plan of Ballindaloch House by AMMS

The Ballindalloch staff at the Summer House (courtesy of Mrs Jessie Dolling)

tumulus occupied the prime site, the castle builders had maintained a respectful distance, but to the Coopers, the mound held no significance and was just an ugly heap of earth so they did not hesitate to have it flattened. With the prospect of creating a superior family home, Henry and Mary had both sites cleared in order to build anew.

The railway had arrived in 1856 and brought Balfron into the modern age. With the station only a mile and a half from the village, it became possible to be in Glasgow in just over an hour. The construction work at Ballindalloch was greatly assisted as transporting stone by rail was relatively cheap with only a short haul from the station by horse and cart. Thus

Henry Cooper was able to build his house in sandstone, probably quarried in Dumfriesshire, backed up by redundant red sandstone from the former castle.

The Coopers' new mansion was built with crow-step gables and stone dormer windows like those on their former house. The style was restrained with stark walls flanking a tower-like entrance which might have belonged to a fortress, but the rooms inside were welcoming and gracefully proportioned with tall windows to capture the magnificent views. Furthermore, the house was beautifully finished with workmanship and materials which hardly deteriorated over the next hundred years, but Henry and Mary did not call it 'Ballindalloch Castle'.

There was plenty of scope for entertaining and ample space for visiting carriages to turn and park on a wide approach like an airport runway. On the garden front, French windows opened onto a terrace where stone steps led down to the lawn. While the menfolk pursued country sports, the ladies could take the air on gravel walks or pick flowers and fruit in the sheltered walled garden. On warm afternoons, tea would be served in the rustic pavilion overlooking the lawn.

Tennis parties took place on a grass court in front of the house. Ballindalloch may have been a founder member of the Inter-house Tennis Club which started in 1888 and is still flourishing. The rules decree that the houses, not their inmates, should be members of the club and the houses were originally required to be within a carriage drive of one another.

To run the house and estate a substantial staff was required. In addition to the usual male and female domestic servants there would at times have been a nursery nurse, governess, laundress and sewing

maid. Coachmen and grooms would have been employed as well as gardeners, gamekeepers, farm workers and foresters, who would have lived with their families on the estate or in tied houses in the village.

On Grassom's map of 1817 (page 101) the south avenue was the main approach to the house, but the advent of the railway caused the north avenue to gain importance. With the station just over a mile away there were frequent journeys with family, visitors and luggage. The North Lodge and gateway were built in 1895.

The Coopers planted lime trees on the north avenue which have since been felled, but many have regenerated. During their time the house was hung with creepers and the two great oaks which still dominate the west lawn were already mature. Hybrid rhododendrons were planted along with beds of roses and massed spring bulbs. Both Samuel and Henry planted trees on parkland and avenues, including the great Wellingtonia south of the garden.

Henry and Mary Cooper enjoyed their mansion for fourteen years, then Henry died in 1882 and Mary followed six years later. If they had hoped their descendants at Ballindalloch would live as they had done, they would have been disappointed because none of their three sons established a family home there. Henry, the eldest, inherited the estate but married late and died childless at the age of 60. Gerald, the youngest, had by then died unmarried. William had followed the path of other younger sons and sought his fortune abroad. In Australia, he had married Matilda Clarke who was, like his mother, of Irish descent and the couple had three daughters. He found adventure serving in the Australian Expeditionary Force in the South African War. When he unexpectedly inherited Ballindalloch at the age of 56, William Cooper returned to Scotland on his own and lived the life of a country gentleman. Fishing the Endrick gave him pleasure, especially when poaching his neighbours' beats. He was regarded as a 'character' and his family remembered him as 'Bill of Ballindalloch'.[5]

The drastic upheaval of World War I put an end to it all and the house had been let for some years when he died in 1920. Both of his surviving daughters had settled abroad. Dorothy had married Charles Witherington, a tea planter in Assam and Amy and her husband, Eric Pitt, lived in Sydney. After 122 years of Cooper ownership, the estate was eventually sold by the heirs of Bill of Ballindalloch.

The sales brochure of 1922 stated 'The mansion House, which is in excellent order, consists of three storeys and contains entrance and inner halls, dining-room, drawing-room, library, billiard-room, thirteen family bedrooms (two being sometimes used as dressing-rooms), five servants' rooms, two bathrooms and ample miscellaneous accommodation. Water from the Glasgow Corporation main from Loch Katrine which passes close to the Estate, is laid on to the Mansion House and Offices.

19th-century dress code for Ballindalloch gentry

The public-room windows overlook a beautiful flower-garden, in which is situated an attractive summer-house, and command fine views of the Campsie Fells. There is also a good lawn-tennis court.'

The Farm and Stables consisted of an 'eight-stalled stable, two loose-boxes, harness-room, large double garage, coachman's and groom's houses, byre, hen-house and dog kennels etc.' Also advertised were the two Lodges, the shootings, the fishings and forty-five acres of woodlands. The farms offered for sale were Ballindalloch, Keirhill, Meikle or Wester Camoquhill and Glenfoot, which was separate from the others. The properties in Balfron Village were Ibertlands, Orchardlands and 17 other houses which were not identified by name or street number.

Like sales brochures today, the deficiencies were glossed over or omitted. There was clearly no electricity, telephone or central heating in the house although the garage was heated with hot-water pipes. There is no mention of gas but it is almost certain that there was a gas plant at the stables and that it was piped from there.

Bill Cooper's sister Cecilia married her cousin from Failford, Alexander Cooper WS, a lawyer with the family firm Cooper and Brodie of Edinburgh. Another sister, Marie was the only daughter of the Ballindalloch family to remain single. Having lived in style, she spent her declining years at Dunibert, an Edwardian villa on the edge of Balfron where she could continue to enjoy an ever changing view of the Campsie Fells. Kay Cameron, nee Donaldson, remembered Miss Cooper as 'a beautiful old lady'.

CHAPTER 9

THE DONALDSON FAMILY

In 1922 Ballindalloch was bought by Norman Donaldson, shipowner of the Donaldson Line. This successful family business had been started by his enterprising father and uncle when the former was only twenty years old and it grew to become one of Britain's major shipping companies. Operating from Glasgow, the principal lines were passenger and cargo to Canada and cargo to South America.

Like Bill of Ballindalloch, young Norman Donaldson served his country in South Africa during the Boer War. After the war he married Catherine, daughter of John Fraser of Balfunning.[1] Their wedding took place in Balfunning House with

Norman Donaldson CBE 1878–1955

Catherine Donaldson
(photograph by Compton Collier)

58

Farm workers and outside staff at the stables

guests seated in the hall as the bride and groom made their vows beneath the stained glass window on the landing of the fine double staircase. Norman and Catherine who was known to her friends as Cassie were blessed with three children – Kay, Graham and Mary.

Before the Donaldsons bought the Ballindalloch estate with its two lodges, stables and Keirhill Farm, they had rented Lettre Cottage with Westerton Farm near Killearn from the Duntreath estate. Norman's two sisters, the Misses Mary and Margaret Donaldson, had meanwhile rented Ballindalloch from the Coopers, before they inherited Aucheneden.[2] From family visits Norman and Cassie already knew Ballindalloch well.

From their new home Norman commuted by train or car to his office in Glasgow. In his spare time he continued to farm and to breed a fine herd of Aberdeen Angus cattle. He would have been proud to call it the Ballindalloch Herd but that name had been taken by Ballindalloch Castle on Speyside where the oldest Aberdeen Angus herd had already been registered. Donaldson's Balfron Herd competed at cattle shows and soon achieved international acclaim. A friendly connection with Cooper descendants was continued in Australia when a famous bull called Elphinstone of Balfron was exported in 1933 to the prize winning Kahula Herd. In due course his Balfron blood could be found in Aberdeen Angus studs throughout New South Wales and Victoria.[3] Robert Minter, a lawyer, whose father owned the celebrated bull, married Jeanette Pitt, a grand-daughter of Bill of Ballindalloch.

Donaldson was a successful race horse owner and celebrated his greatest triumph when Musadora won the Oaks in 1951. He was also a keen horseman and sportsman, who enjoyed fishing and shooting. When the family arrived at Ballindalloch the garden was almost surrounded by trees so a large number were felled. A subsequent gale flattened many more but, undismayed, they made the most of the view and began to plan innovations. Being

Prize bull of the Balfron Herd

Norman Donaldson leading in Musadora *after winning The Oaks in 1951*

a dedicated gardener Cassie kept a diary and recorded developments. She planted Atlantic cedars, rhododendrons, fruit trees, acers and several varieties of holly which still produce bountiful berries for decking the halls. A new green-house was built and next to the walled garden a new border was made. The Coopers' rose beds were removed when Cassie created a rectangular rose garden surrounded by a castellated yew hedge.

By this time the Ballindalloch Cotton Mill had closed, so she obtained redundant flagstones and used them to pave the terrace walk next to the house, where stone troughs and urns were filled with plants to give colour. As a lover of beautiful things Cassie considered tennis courts extremely unsightly, especially the grass court in front of their house. The problem was solved by concealing a hard court in the wood where it could not be an eyesore. Thereafter, family cricket matches were played on the lawn and marquees were erected there to celebrate weddings.

Ballindalloch House had hardly altered since it was built but Norman and

Cassie arrived with fresh ideas to brighten their new home. The drawing room was given a lift with an oak parquet floor and an Adam style mantelpiece with a basket grate. Ornate embellishments on the overhead plasterwork were replaced by more delicate corner motifs which have since been recreated in the present house. Pitch pine floors were laid throughout the hall, morning room and dining room where connecting doors formed a suite for entertaining. Upstairs, the number of bathrooms was conveniently increased.

Between the wars the era of gracious living continued for the residents of country houses. While still in bed they would be pleasantly awakened with tea while a housemaid opened the curtains, cleared the grate and lit the bedroom fire. For morning ablutions a can of steaming hot water would be delivered for use with the china ewer and basin on the wash stand. In the servants' quarters, stone floors echoed with summoning bells and the answering clatter of feet. Each morning the lady of the house would meet with cook to discuss the menus of the day. Meals were announced by the sound of a gong and evening wear would be laid out in readiness for the family to change for dinner. Observing a strict hierarchy below stairs the staff also waited upon each other.

This labour intensive style of living provided abundant employment, but back-stair journeys with buckets of coal decreased with the advent of central heating. At Ballindalloch a coal fired boiler was installed with a four inch diameter main pipe to feed about 30 radiators. The system was later converted to oil with a 9000 litre tank which was probably built for a Donaldson ship. Gas was replaced by electricity supplied from a generator at the stables. When mains electricity eventually arrived, the meter for Ballindalloch house was at the stables and it has remained there ever since.

Domestic life was improved by the electric iron, vacuum cleaner and refrigerator, not to mention the wireless and the gramophone. The telephone had reached the village by 1922 and the Ballindalloch number began as 'Balfron 2'. Norman and Cassie both acquired motor cars and each of them employed a chauffeur. Cassie called hers 'my motor man'. Estate and farm workers occupied Ballindalloch properties while domestic staff were at the big house. The servants' hall was a cheerful retreat where George Formby and Arthur Askey provided entertainment 'on the air'. There were games of Snap and Old Maid, cheeky postcards from Blackpool and a printed invitation to the 'Young Mens' Dance' at Buchlyie where black ties were to be worn.[4] Each Sunday, Jimmy Simpson the joiner called to wind all the clocks and was invariably rewarded with a meal from Phemie the cook.

During the 1930s Ballindalloch celebrated three Donaldson weddings. First, Kay married Ewen Cameron and then, in 1936 Graham wed Johan Mitchell. That year there was further rejoicing when

The wedding at Balfron Kirk of Mary Donaldson and Noël Carrington-Smith in 1936

Mary became the wife of a Canadian, Noel Carrington-Smith. The younger generation soon set up homes and began to raise their families nearby, but everything changed in September 1939 when the outbreak of World War II disrupted their lives. Within 24 hours a passenger liner, the Donaldson flagship *Athenia*, was torpedoed and sunk by a German U Boat. From then on the Donaldson shipping company was faced with grave responsibilities while the industry struggled to provide ships to bring in essential supplies.

Like other young families the Donaldsons were torn apart when the three men left their wives and children to go and fight the war. Mary sailed overseas with hers to join Noel's parents in Canada while her siblings' families remained in and around Ballindalloch. Kay's family moved into the nursery flat while Johan's took up residence at Ballindalloch Stables before renting the Old Manse.

While young men left jobs and homes to serve in the forces and women went to work in canteens, hospitals and factories, many country houses were requisitioned or required to house evacuees. Near Balfron, Ballikinrain Castle became a girls' school.[5] Though the blackout and rationing caused formidable changes, Ballindalloch managed to remain intact to survive the war with the aid a few faithful servants. In the garden, flower beds were turned into vegetable plots while uncut lawns were used for hen runs and grazing for livestock. Cassie enjoyed keeping hens and her extended household preserved eggs and fruit while making the most of produce from the estate.

The women folk at Ballindalloch joined their neighbours in the village, knitting comforts for the troops and organising whist drives, jumble sales and raffles to raise funds for the war effort. Cassie served on the Red Cross and the Balfron Church Guild and, after Mary departed, Kay and Johan continued to run the Girl Guides.

Norman Donaldson, while supervising work on the farm as well as the Donaldson Line, also did his bit for Balfron when he joined *Dad's Army* and served as Company Commander of the Home Guard. Luckily, no wartime disaster occurred in Strathendrick though there was a scare in September 1940 when Donaldson was suddenly alerted with the code-word 'Cromwell' indicating that a German invasion was imminent.[6] In some areas the Home Guard was called out by ringing church bells. Poor Cassie was alarmed by a phone call from her husband and is said to have rushed to warn Johan at the Stables bearing frantic instructions 'Drive the cattle before you to Aucheneden!' These momentous words became a family legend. If there had been a plan to emulate Rob Roy by hiding the herd in a

nearby canyon known to locals as the Whangie, the truth may never be known since the panic, like many other wartime dramas, turned out to be a false alarm.

While hostilities continued overseas, Ewen Cameron became a prisoner of war. Graham Donaldson was recalled from the army and thereafter travelled regularly to London to serve at the Ministry of Shipping. During this arduous period he became seriously ill and in 1945 he died, leaving Johan with three young sons. After the war the Camerons went to live at Aucheneden which they inherited from their Donaldson aunts. The Carrington-Smiths settled in Perthshire while Johan and her family remained in Balfron. By then taxation was penal and labour in short supply. Phemie the cook and Mrs Cockley the housekeeper loyally stayed on at Ballindalloch and were later joined by Fraser the butler. When the ever fastidious Cassie apologised to Fraser for having been too hard on him he replied, 'Think nothing of it ma'am, when I was in the army I served under a very difficult sergeant.'

The garden at Ballindalloch never regained its pre-war state but the ornamental trees which the Donaldsons had planted were growing up to create a new landscape. The post war years were hard times for the Donaldson Line and the whole of the shipping industry. Norman Donaldson was Company Chairman from 1941 until he retired in 1948. He died in 1955 and has been commemorated by a plaque in Balfron Church. His death was soon followed by that of Cassie, his widow. The Donaldson family have contributed generously to the community of Balfron, and Donaldson Park continues to play an important part in the life of the village.

The Ballindalloch estate was split up and Keirhill farm was sold. Ballindalloch House with four and a half acres was bought by John Glen and the southern part of the Stable block was bought with four acres by Murray and Marian Scrimgeour. The Donaldson family continued to own the fields, the woods, the two lodges and the rest of the stable steading which is known as Ballindalloch Farm Cottage.

In 1954 Johan married John Dunlop and, with their daughter Mary, the family lived for many years at Camoqhill Douglas.[7] Johan was a keen sportswoman

and a joint founder of Riding for the Disabled in Scotland. In 1967 her son, John Donaldson, having served with the Queen's Own Highlanders, bought back Keirhill and combined it with the land at Ballindalloch to make a viable farm. He married Charlotte Munro of Foulis in 1975 and they had three children. After John's illness and death in 1985 Char managed the farm and later served as Chairman of Scotland's Gardens Scheme. In 1992 she married Lt. Col. Robin Hunt who had also been bereaved. His two children were a welcome addition to the family at Keirhill which became the parental home of them all.

When John Dunlop suddenly died in 1974 Johan was widowed again and continued to take a kindly interest in the village of Balfron where she spent the final years before she died in 1999.

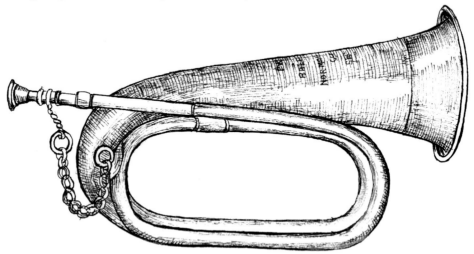

September 1940
A bugle was inscribed and presented to Balfron Home Guard by Norman P. Donaldson CBE Co. Com.
The bugler was Robert Wilson, Shoemaker of Balfron.

CHAPTER 10

THE GLEN FAMILY

When Ballindalloch House was offered for sale it might have had a different future. After World War II the Trustees of the Burrell Collection had been actively seeking a smoke and fog-free home for the Museum. For about forty years after Sir William Burrell[1] donated his Collection to the City of Glasgow, his treasures could not be shown to the public because his deed of gift had stipulated that they must not be exposed to urban pollution. A site wass required at least 16 miles from the city centre and within 4 miles of Killearn.[2] Ballindalloch was seriously considered but, in the end nothing came of it. When the Clean Air Act took effect the Glasgow atmosphere was purified and a fine new building in Pollok Park provided the solution.

In 1958 John Glen bought Ballindalloch House and a family connection continued because his wife Jill was related to the Donaldsons. He had retired from running a Glasgow company which supplied waterproof clothing but later he became involved in other business interests. He launched into a new career in 1970 by standing for Parliament as Conservative candidate for the West Stirlingshire constituency. Although not elected he was able to achieve a notable reduction in the Labour majority. As a regular rifle shooting competitor at Bisley, John won four major trophies and for several years was successful in captaining the Scottish team.

John and Jill had three sons, Jonathan, Angus and Simon, who were brought up at Ballindalloch. Enormous changes had taken place during and since the war and the cost of employing staff had become increasingly expensive. Many households now relied on daily help, but raising a young family in a large house could not easily be done single handed so, for eight years, Jill employed a living in cook and also enlisted a succession of 'au pair' girls to help look after the children.

Although the staff which once filled the servants' hall no longer existed,

1970, John and Jill with Jonathan, Angus and Simon with Linty the labrador.

Ballindalloch was as lively as ever because the Glens made the most of their big house and filled it with people. As the children grew up the household increased until more than a dozen were often in residence. Jill's sister, Jean Drapper, moved in with her two young sons. Alistair and Elspeth Paterson rented the nursery flat on the top floor for seventeen years and Elspeth's mother came to join them. Furthermore the cook had a young son, Robert Reid, who now lives in Balfron. Over at the stables the Scrimgeours had five children including another three boys

so John Glen had no difficulty raising a cricket eleven. The predominance of males was better balanced when, from time to time, the Patersons were visited by twin god-daughters.

Ballindalloch has always been a great place for the young so the children were able to enjoy it all. With an endless supply of trees to climb and a burn for falling in the boys had plenty of scope for wild games. One of their ploys was using the house as a climbing frame and shinning up drain pipes and crow-steps to the top of the roof. The parents of some visitors were more than a little disturbed on learning that their offspring had spent a jolly afternoon pretending to be steeplejacks. When the Glen boys followed family tradition and took up rifle shooting with their father, there was keen target practice and they soon became excellent shots by culling the Ballindalloch rabbits.

The Glens' 4½ acres needed a lot of maintenance because much of it consisted of lawn which had been reclaimed after the war. Three acres of grass needed regular mowing so John soon acquired the necessary mowers and the wide green swards became his pride and joy. Jill was involved in raising funds for the British Sailors Society and the lawns made a perfect venue for charity functions. John and Jill also hosted events for the Conservative Association.

To enhance the ambience at Ballindalloch peacocks were procured, but John had trouble persuading them to parade on his lawns because the ungrateful birds kept wandering off to the woods and even turned up in the village. The village children were rewarded with tips for finding lost peacocks and herding them home but the cost of recovery became exorbitant when all the pupils of Balfron Primary School claimed to have found a peacock simultaneously and each one demanded the full reward.

The shrubbery beyond the west lawn had become a wilderness, so John fenced it off and turned to rearing pheasants. He enjoyed fishing the Endrick and, as Ballin-

dalloch was close at hand for a quick dash to the river bank when conditions were right, his salmon rod was made up ready and suspended from hooks near the back door.

John and Jill brought Ballindalloch up to date by adapting rooms for new purposes and bringing the garden nearer the house. The old dining room became an enormous play room with an enclosed stove. The kitchen was completely refurbished in pine with a wall full of cupboards, and a door was knocked out to the garden. The old laundry became a garden shed and the former servants' hall was turned into a garage for John's lawn mowers. Upstairs, decking was built so that the Patersons could have a roof garden where they could sit out and enjoy the view among the pots and tubs which Elspeth filled with a riot of plants. The billiard room was divided to make John's office, which was known to the family as 'No 10'.

In the garden, the grass bank west of the house was replaced by long stepped terraced beds with stone retaining walls. Then the terrace was given an Italian look by replacing the Victorian steps with a wider flight flanked by cypresses. The paved terrace walk was edged with a low stone wall topped by wide slabs which could be used as a seat. Plants could now be grown near to the house and enjoyed from the windows throughout the year. After the new terrace beds were established the Donaldson rose garden was grassed over and used as a putting green.

With minimal help in the garden the work load became difficult to sustain and, as time went on, the house demanded increasing maintenance. The place was becoming a burden and John and Jill were beginning to flag. After nineteen happy years it was a wrench for them to leave, but when their family grew up and began to flee the nest they decided that a smaller house would be more appropriate and made up their minds to build one. In 1976 John and Jill sold Ballindalloch House and moved to Brig o' Turk.

Ballindalloch House from the west by SMOS 1977

CHAPTER 11

THE STEPHEN FAMILY

The final chapters concern the recent owners whose claim to be 'history' is dubious, and whether this part of the story should now be 'lost' is entirely up to the reader. As this record of the Stephen venture may have some aspects which are less interesting than others, the sections have headings so that there is no need to waste time in reading all, or indeed any of it.

New Owners

In 1976 Alexander Stephen became the owner of Ballindalloch and eyebrows were raised when it became known that he and his wife intended to knock down most of the house. Sandy and Sue were not normally inclined to such recklessness. For twenty-two years they had lived in an old whitewashed cottage in Houston in Renfrewshire and would have been happy to remain there if developers had not changed the village into a satellite town. Serious house hunting had begun in 1973.

The Long Hunt

They had hoped for another cottage somewhere safe from developers – a farmhouse or an old manse. Almost at once a potentially ideal home was found, but after a year of plans and negotiations, Sandy and Sue were devastated when the project had to be abandoned. After that more than fifty properties were inspected but none came up to the mark. Three came on the market twice and one of them was Ballindalloch. The glossy brochure advertising 'A fine Baronial Mansion House, suitable for conversion to flats, a country club or hotel' had been instantly rejected, but two years later a second advertisement prompted further investigation. Sandy and Sue were captivated by the setting. The house was far too big but the two-storey wing was not unlike the kind of dwelling they had hoped for. The wild idea of demolishing two thirds of a massive country house would have been discarded out of hand had the Stephens not been desperate.

Fortunately Ballindalloch was not a

Aerial view 1977 (courtesy of RCAHMS)

listed building. Frank Bracewell, Senior Planner of Stirling Council, gave approval in principle to the plan and a quantity surveyor was consulted to ensure the scheme was viable. After considerable financial and technical machinations the house with 4½ acres was bought from John Glen. In addition the walled garden and an acre at the front of the house were bought from the Donaldsons through Johan Dunlop who was related to both Sue and Sandy.

Reasons and Reactions

The Donaldsons were kind and supportive, and if they mourned the fate of their former family home, the Stephens heard

nothing of it. To others it may have seemed like vandalism to destroy the 'Big Hoose' of Balfron, but the Victorian mansion was unsuited to modern living. The rooms were spacious and elegant but the cost of living in them had become

The drawing room before demolition (courtesy of RCAHMS)

exorbitant. Parts of the house were dark and damp and the back stairs were lethal. Housework was a nightmare with seven different types of electric socket. And there was dry rot. Re-roofing and re-wiring, modernising plumbing and central heating plus re-decoration would have cost far more than it did to create a smaller and more practical house.

Background

Sandy Stephen was a shipbuilder. His family firm, Alexander Stephen and Sons, had been founded in Burghead in 1750 and Stephen yards were established in Aberdeen, Arbroath and Dundee before Sandy's great-great-grandfather moved his company to Glasgow in 1850 to concentrate on building iron ships. The Stephens

built almost a thousand ships including passenger ships, cargo liners, warships and tankers. One ship which came to the public notice during the Falklands War was the Royal Fleet Auxiliary *Sir Galahad* which was savaged by the Argentinian Air Force in Bluff Cove. The Linthouse ship-yard prospered until the 1960s but when the British shipbuilding industry collapsed, the yard had to be closed and the Company was wound up in 1983. Sandy was also a Director of Scottish Widows Life Assurance and the Murray Investment Trusts. In his capacity as an engineer he became a Governor of the Glasgow School of Art to the amusement of Sue who had trained at the rival establishment, the Edinburgh College of Art. She too came from shipbuilding stock, her great-

ABOVE LEFT. Shenandoah, *the notorious Confederate raider in the American Civil War. Built by Stephens in 1863.*
ABOVE. *In 1947 the Stephen built corvette HMS* Amethyst *was seriously damaged by Chinese communist batteries on the* Yangtse *river and made a dramatic escape to the sea. The story was retold in the film 'Yangtse Incident' starring Richard Todd.*
LEFT. SS Australasian *built by J & G Thomson in 1857 for the European and Australian Royal Mail Company.*

71

grandfather having co-founded J & G Thomson which later became John Brown of Clydebank.

From his Stephen forbears Sandy had inherited a strong tradition in International Yacht Racing. He and Sue continued the trend by competing for two decades in the International Dragon Class. In 1968 they came close to selection for the Mexico Olympics. The intensive teamwork was good training for the life they would lead at Ballindalloch.

Arrival

The Stephens moved to Ballindalloch in September 1976 and though their chil-

dren were reluctant to be uprooted they took a tolerant view of the mad parental scheme. Graham, Zannah and Sacha were then aged 20, 16 and 13. There was plenty of space at Ballindalloch, but no domestic help, so all the cleaning was done by Sue. Although the task was formidable the house was ready to welcome the girls when they came home for half term. For the first year life was relatively civilised and they managed to live more or less like normal people.

Measuring

As Sandy's commitments decreased he was able to work part time on the house.

1977 Sandy and Sue with Graham, Zannah and Sacha and Juno the spaniel.

Being a naval architect he could design and draw his own plans so no Architect was employed. The original plans of the house had been lost so they had to be redrawn. On a wet November afternoon he and Sue went outside and started to measure the house. Sue held the linen tape aloft with raindrops trickling up her sleeve while Sandy wrote down the measurements on a soggy piece of paper. Later, he was mystified to discover that one side of the house appeared to be longer than the other. The linen tape had stretched in the rain so next day they bought a steel one.

Planning Permission

The scheme entailed knocking off twenty five rooms by demolishing the main three-storey building with only the two-storey servants' quarters retained. The smaller house was to be made symmetrical by adding five rooms, using existing stonework and the smaller doors and windows from the upper storeys of the mansion. It took nine months to draw the plans and submit them to Stirling Council. The Planning Department and Building Control had been helpful when consulted and when the plans were submitted no alterations were required.

Experts from Historic Scotland, the Glasgow Civic Trust and even the Georgian Society came to give advice on altering the Victorian house. Although they agreed that it had no significant historic or architectural merit, they admired the materials and craftsmanship

and advised the Stephens to re-use as much as possible. Planning permission was granted in June 1977.

Moving to the Back Quarters

Winter created arctic conditions when the heating system was dismantled. Windows became spangled with frost and the cloak-room loo filled up with icebergs. The electrician laughed at Sue for wearing a coat inside her own house to which she retorted 'You're mistaken Frank. I'm wearing two.' Having contemplated a mobile home, the family chose to stay put and camp in the back quarters. 173 sacks and boxes were labelled and stacked up to the ceilings, so each room was like a furniture van with minimal living space inside. Only basic necessities were kept for everyday use.

The temporary staircase was used for more than a year

73

The family adapted to their new quarters and learned to live with plaster dust infiltrating their clothes, hair and even food while pneumatic hammers reverberated just beyond their walls. After withstanding the first sharp shocks they grew accustomed to the sound of crashing masonry. Both staircases had to be demolished and, for more than a year, the only way to get upstairs to the bathroom and the children's rooms was by a ladder, though the climb became easier when Sandy installed some engine room steps. The kitchen made a cosy living room and Sandy and Sue slept next door in the old ironing room among stacks of furniture. After living all over the house the family enjoyed being near together. With their surplus belongings stashed away they sometimes wondered why they had them in the first place. There was nowhere to have a party so Sacha celebrated her sixteenth birthday with 35 friends who came with tents and spent the weekend camping in the garden and jiving to a disco in a do-it-yourself marquee.

The front of the house looked like a builders' yard so visitors could hardly believe that people were living inside. It was looking excessively sordid when the rating inspector turned up. After a tour of the house he had no hesitation in declaring Ballindalloch unfit for habitation and therefore exempt from rates. All the family became involved in the alterations and, in spite of the inconvenience, the noise and the filth, the anxiety and the exhaustion, their life in the kitchen turned out to be an amazingly happy time. Friends were invited to come and see the 'progress' because, whatever the outcome, the experience was so extraordinary that Sandy and Sue felt at least some of it ought to be shared. When life at Ballindalloch became

Sandy lifting the Donaldson floor boards. Instructions to demolishers were drawn on the walls.

totally chaotic Sue's mother confided to a friend 'The funny thing is they seem to enjoy it!'

Dismantling

Everything required for re-use was carefully listed and stored. It was hard to find enough sheds and outhouses to accommodate the stacks of doors, windows, shutters, skirting boards, mantelpieces, door knobs and stair rods along with mirrors and bathroom fittings. Sandy lifted 900 square feet of pitch pine flooring finding 'Donaldson Line' written on some of the planks. Sue dismantled 14 mantelpieces and chipped rows of plaster acanthus leaves from high ceiling cornices. Together they lifted, numbered and boxed 2,500 pieces of oak parquet flooring from the drawing room. Later on, Sandy constructed a caustic-soda tank in the back yard where he and Sue, clad in

Sue in protective gear. She dismantled 14 fireplaces.

oilskins and wellies, stripped 27 panelled doors. When Sue complained of a bad back Dr Keighley said 'Don't worry. You'll finish up with a perfect house and a back like a stevedore'.

Demolition

The ghastly deed of destruction was undertaken by Burnthills of Johnstone who completed the task in six weeks. An enormous yellow JCB named *Big Wullie* trundled up the avenue, then a fearsome gang turned up, armed with picks and crowbars. They swarmed over the roof using the crow-steps as stairs and stripped off hundreds of slates which they stacked in front of the house. *Big Wullie's* bucket was used as a lift and the young Stephens managed to hitch a ride. John Gallacher, the foreman, heaved hunks of stone as if they were brickbats. Pieces of masonry required for rebuilding were carefully laid out on the front lawn and chimney pots were used as goal posts when the men played football during their lunch break. Juno, the spaniel, hunted after their 'pieces' and a label had to be hung on her collar saying 'Please do not feed me: I have a weight problem.' *Big Wullie* reduced the building to rubble and shovelled it into heaps. The house disappeared as the walls crumbled and crashed in clouds of dust until the site looked like a scene from the Blitz. It was disconcerting for Sandy and Sue to see their assets in ruins and realise they no longer possessed a viable house.

Demolition took 6 weeks but reconstruction continued for several years.

The wreckers

Billy Scott

Rebuilding

As the house was dismantled homes were found for many items which could not be re-used. Pine mantelpieces were popular with family and friends, and the iron balusters from the back stairs found a new life in the restoration of Mains of Glynn. The main contractor was Scotts of Balfron and it was a happy arrangement employing a family firm with Jock Scott, Billy and Alastair. The team included Andy Dunn, John MacKay, Scott Benson, Kenneth Jackson, Duncan Marshall and Robert Reid. Frank Farquharson was the steadfast electrician as well as the Stephens' elder at Balfron Kirk. He was ever ready with a joke, even when a ceiling fell down. Gardiner of Blanefield served as plumbers and heating engineers, with Alan Muir faithfully fitting a snakes' honeymoon of pipes.

Every effort was made to re-use original materials. By re-fitting existing dormers and crow-steps, traditional features used in both of the former houses were retained.

New rooms began to take shape and, best of all, a staircase. It was designed by Sandy, with treads and risers made from the pitch pine flooring, while Sue designed scrolled ends for the steps. Cast iron balusters from the main staircase were put back into use but, having been made for a different stair, they ended with several 'deliberate mistakes' for observant visitors to spot. Juno who had been confined to the ground floor for more than a year, was suddenly able to bound upstairs and discover a whole new world.

Though care went into choosing the decorative plaster work the drawing room ceiling ended by inadvertently combining

Scotts working on the new extension.

Alastair Scott and Andy Dunn building the new staircase with recycled components.

the styles of three different periods. The 'glass' cupola over the staircase was actually double glazed plastic. As details did not always turn out as intended, Sue learned the art of faking with paint and stain. Photographs she had taken before the demolition proved to be very helpful. She also ordered stacks of panel moulding to create an authentic impression with dummy picture rails and shutters.

During their holidays Zannah and Sacha helped, and Graham, about to start his career in computers, apprenticed himself to the plumber and the electrician. Before long he was able to make a valuable contribution and the experience has served him ever since. He was soon receiving dinner invitations from young ladies requesting 'By the way Graham, please bring your tools'.

Willy Thomson plastering the cupola.

Sandy restoring cornices.

Decorating

As no professionals were employed the family had to work for years, but young James Mackenzie came for a weekend visit and stayed for a month to help. Sue worked for eleven days to paper the hall, passages, landing and stairs, though the twenty foot drop above the staircase turned out to be a precarious ladder operation with three members of the family working at different levels. Decorating turned out to be one of the most tiring jobs but luckily the girls were keen to do up their own rooms. Zannah spent a week working on hers and when she stripped the old paper off she found the signature of the decorator who had pasted it there for the Donaldsons in 1923. She copied him, writing 'This paper was hung by Zannah Stephen in April 1980 – and I hope I never see this bit of wall again!'

A new room became habitable about every six weeks. In the drawing room two thousand pieces of the oak parquet flooring were re-laid, sanded and waxed. Recycled woodwork was fitted by joiners

and the finer plaster work was installed by George Rome of Glasgow. Meanwhile Sandy fitted cornices in the master bedroom, dressing room and the back passage. The acanthus leaves which Sue had collected were reassembled in strips by Sandy and Sacha to complete the cornices in the upstairs rooms. Sue altered 22 curtains and manufactured many more while Sandy laid a patchwork of recycled carpets. In June 1984 the Stephens were able to enjoy the fruits of their labours and celebrate with a midsummer dance for Zannah and Sacha.

The New House

Although two decades went by before the last attic cupboard was painted, the house with three public rooms and six bedrooms was virtually complete five years after moving in. Most rooms were modest in size, the biggest being the drawing room at 23 feet by 16½ feet. Original windows were repositioned to make the most of the views and the sun. In the back yard, the old dairy, larder, boiler house and outside

Garden view from the north-west.

loo were turned into a small guest cottage which connected with the house so it could be used either by house guests or independent visitors. Later, Johan Dunlop lived in Dairy Cottage for six months while her future abode in the village was being altered. She enjoyed inviting her friends to play bridge and showing them the bedroom which had once been her father-in-law's boiler house.

Ballindalloch became a flexible house which adapted to many purposes, not only for family and friends but also for charities and good causes. With ingenuity, by shifting furniture and borrowing tables and chairs, surprisingly large numbers of people could be welcomed and after the alterations Ballindalloch could still provide beds for fourteen people.[1]

The Family

While the developments were going on, Sacha had left school. She worked as a chalet girl and as a secretary. In London she studied cookery with Pru Leith and began a career in catering. In 1985, when aged twenty-two, Sacha was on her way to work when her bicycle was hit by a lorry and she died as a result of the accident. Sandy and Sue had already lost their infant daughter Alice in 1959, and after this second tragedy the family took a long time to recover.

But life must go on. Later that year Graham was happily married in Switzerland to Beatrix Balsiger, known as Trix. Soon there were three Stephen grand-daughters – Jessica, Fiona and Melanie. After that Ballindalloch was often visited by grandchildren and dogs. Sue's 60th birthday party was held in the garden and gleeful children queued for custard pies to throw at Sandy. There were winter sledging parties and a gorgeous litter of 8 spaniel pups. Trix organised a tennis school for the young ones and the place came alive with people enjoying themselves.

Having graduated from St Andrews University Zannah worked for Sotheby's in Glasgow and London, but after her sister died she gave up her job and spent a year back-packing. When she came home she became a landscape architect, and settled in Edinburgh. Sandy and Sue were glad to have all the family in Scotland again, but Zannah still loved to travel. In 1997 a third disaster struck when, at the age of thirty-seven, she was drowned in a diving accident during a tour of South America. The loss of a third daughter was almost unbearable.

The following year Sandy had a big operation for cancer. The outlook was far from good but he made a remarkable recovery. Thanks to the loving support of family and friends he and Sue were able to keep going and find peace in the garden, fields and woods. Working outside was the best therapy and the healing power of Ballindalloch gradually renewed their spirits. There were more happy times with grandchildren and gatherings of friends and relations while Sandy and Sue found endless joy tending and sharing Ballindalloch.

Family group 2001. Sandy and Sue with Graham and Trix, Jessica, Fiona and Melanie.

CHAPTER 12

THE GOOD LIFE

Knocking down and rebuilding a house was a major project, but outside another big challenge lay in wait. Sandy and Sue had loved the garden from the start because sunshine and shelter combine to

The Terrace Walk

give Ballindalloch a sense of peace and a climate of its own. When cold winds whip through the streets of Balfron, the garden can be bathed in warmth with wagtails darting about the lawns and butterflies sunning themselves on the terrace. The place is a haven for wildlife as well as for people who live there. Time and again the Stephens would arrive home from a holiday, look about them and wonder why they ever went away.

For more than ten years no help was employed in the house or the garden. The first five years at Ballindalloch had been devoted to working on the house and only basic maintenance of the 6½ acres had been possible. The next stage seemed formidable until Lady Macmillan of Finlaystone advised 'Start near the house and work outwards'.

The Terrace

Sue armed herself with a kitchen knife and spent weeks clearing broken glass and rubble from the paved Terrace Walk.

When she was finally able to introduce plants among the flagstones they grew so abundantly that Graham warned 'If you let a small child go there it might get lost'. In 1982 she and Sandy cleared the terrace beds, an area of fifty square metres, and dug in loads of peat and compost to improve the heavy clay soil. A path of flagstones was laid along the back of each terrace which reduced the cultivated area and made the beds easy to tend. Along the base of the terraces more flagstones were sunk into the lawn to avoid the need to clip grass edges. The raised beds were planted with small shrubs including old fashioned roses and various evergreens interspersed with low plants which needed no staking. Beyond the terrace, Cassie Donaldson's shrubs had reached maturity so, at either end, the colours of her golden hollies and crimson acers were echoed in the new planting. With far less labour the terrace began to look rather like a deep herbaceous border.

The Ruin

On the site of the Bronze Age tumulus, a Ruin Garden was made inside the broken

The Ruin Garden

Ruin planting includes Wisteria 'Pink Ice' and Actinidia kolomikta, Hybrid tea and Floribunda roses.

Wisteria sinensis 'Alba'. Roses 'Alba maxima', climbing 'Iceberg' and 'Pour toi'.

walls of the mansion. It looked south to the Campsie Fells and became an extension of the house. Sue spent the winter of 1981 digging beds and spreading muck till the place stank like a midden. Though they both had back trouble Sandy eventually laid over 600 flagstones. Some slabs rescued from the house were 6 feet long and 4 inches thick.[1] After the walls of the Ruin had been carefully pointed a friend declared them to be insufficiently ruinous,

so Sandy was made to climb up and ruin them again.

Roses and herbaceous plants were introduced in 1982, with some success and plenty of failures. The ruined walls invited climbers, so wisteria and clematis were soon twining through the stone mullions, but this was not a labour saving idea. They had been warned 'Plant climbers and you plant trouble'.

In a corner of the Ruin a White

Garden was made where three walls formed a little courtyard. The centre piece was a bird bath and the planting was done in shades of white – at least that was Sue's intention. Bachelor's buttons, campanula and self seeding daisies romped among the flagstones to fraternize with apple mint and lily of the valley. Silver foliage complemented virginal white roses, tulips, and lilies but plants had a nasty habit of turning up in colours so from time to time there were evictions.

The surplus stone from the demolition was buried south of the Ruin and it took Sandy and Sue 160 man hours to level and seed a lawn. It ended in a steep bank where wild flowers made themselves at home, though invading dandelions, thistles and buttercups were firmly rejected to make way for fox and cubs, speedwell, birdsfoot trefoil and lady's smock.

The Obelisk Sundial

The sundial on the south lawn is an Historic Monument dating from the reign of Charles I. It is a multiple sundial in the form of an obelisk and once bristled with copper gnomen which cast their shadows on sunken dials in various geometric shapes. The gnomen have disintegrated and the markings on the stone have been eroded. Obelisks were fashionable during the 17th century when these curious garden objects came to be highly rated among the nobility. The Ballindalloch sundial might have commemorated the marriage of the 9th Earl of Glencairn which took place in 1637.

Similar sundials still exist at the castles of Stirling, Leckie, Drummond and Kelburn as well as at Auchenbowie, Ballencleroch and Sauchieburn. The Stirling Castle sundial may relate to the visit made by King Charles I after his coronation at Holyrood in 1633. Three years earlier the Drummond Castle obelisk was built for the Earl of Perth by the royal stonemason, John Mylne, and designed to tell the time in different capitals of the world.

The Ballindalloch obelisk once stood

17th century

19th century

21st century

in front of the house on the site of the old castle, but during the 1920s it was damaged by a horse and cart and moved across the avenue. After three years of negotiations with Historic Scotland the Stephens finally had it transferred to their garden in 1996, when three men took three days to shift it thirty yards. There was a small celebration when the sundial was proudly unveiled by Mary Carrington-Smith, who was formerly a Donaldson of Ballindalloch.

The Walled Garden

The date of this garden is not known though walled gardens have existed from medieval times to give protection against the elements, wild life and other unwelcome intruders. At Ballindalloch the massive walls were built of local stone. A

walk once led from the Old House through the orchard where some of the daffodils are known to have been in cultivation during the 17th century.[2] Having for centuries supplied the household with vegetables, fruit and flowers the garden was abandoned after World War II. Christmas trees were grown for a time and since then it has been grazed.

The Tennis Court

As the Donaldsons' tennis court had been abandoned, Sue's mother kindly helped to fund a hard court next to the walled garden. When *Big Wullie*, the JCB, levelled the site, the heap of topsoil was promised for the new Ruin Garden so Sue was not amused when it vanished into the foundations of the tennis court. *Big Wullie* saved the day by using his bucket to excavate an

Anyone for tennis?

Fields and Trees

The mowing was halved when the front lawn became a paddock. The avenue was given curves and cattle grids, and one grid arrived with a tiny escape ramp in case a hedgehog should fall in. Parkland trees were planted as well as daffodils which flower unaffected by grazing livestock. The Stephens increased their property to 80 acres which made a perfect little estate. The fields continued to be farmed by John Donaldson and were later let to Robert Steel and his son David, while Sandy maintained fences, sprayed weeds, trapped moles and cleared fallen timber.

Ballindalloch has grown some magnificent trees. Several oaks pre-date Robert Dunmore, the largest being 23 feet in circumference. The big sprawling yew which stands near the avenue may be the oldest tree in the parish. The tallest tree at Ballindalloch is the giant Wellingtonia which has a massive girth of 33 feet. Some

alternative supply from the walled garden, and the resulting crater served as a garden refuse dump for the next three decades. The tennis court was enjoyed by family and friends, and numerous matches and tournaments were held for the Interhouse Tennis Club.

Snowdrops in the paddock

Old Stables

Farm Cottage

huge beeches on the avenues were planted about 1820. Over 100 mature parkland trees survive from before World War II, and young trees are still being planted.

Lodges, Stables and the Ballindalloch Shoot

The two lodges used to be occupied by staff. Norman Donaldson replaced the old South Lodge with a larger two-storey building in 1926. When the Stephens came to Ballindalloch, the North Lodge was occupied by Sandy MacLean, who was the last Donaldson retainer and still employed. As there were heavy snowfalls then, it was always a joy when he arrived like a knight in armour, with a snow-plough to clear the avenue and let the Stephens get their cars out. Later both lodges were sold and they have since been enlarged. The South Lodge was bought by John and Ros Ford in 1989.[3]

The southern part of the stable block, known as Old Stables, was bought in 1958 by Murray and Marian Scrimgeour who brought up their five children there. The Scrimgeours have long been familiar figures at Ballindalloch, Marian intrepidly pedalling her bike and Murray, busy in overalls sawing up logs. Over the years Marian has made a major contribution to the Met Office by monitoring the local weather and may yet exert her influence to reduce global warming.

Ballindalloch Farm Cottage, has been occupied since the 1970s by Peter and Lois Holmes whose son, Niall, grew up sturdily among a lively collection of dogs, cats and other livestock. In addition to Peter's work as gamekeeper, he and Lois have been actively involved in the breeding, training and showing of gundogs, while delighting Ballindalloch children with generations of puppies.

The Keirhill and Ballindalloch land has made a good small pheasant shoot, keepered by Peter Holmes. A family syndicate was run by John Donaldson till Sandy took over at Ballindalloch for eleven years. Since then it has been organized by Robin and Char Hunt at Keirhill. The shoot is a modest one where friends meet and enjoy the country on foot without inflicting wholesale carnage among the pheasant population.

Teamwork

In 1987 Andrew Brown came to help at Ballindalloch. Thanks to his enthusiasm real progress was made in the garden and the team worked happily together for fifteen years. There were many achievements during this time because Andrew was glad to turn his hand to almost any task.

To cope with the eighty acres, seven internal combustion engines were used. Sandy took an hour and a quarter to mow two acres of lawn with a Wheelhorse tractor pulling triple gang-mowers.

Clearing timber

Andrew took about the same time to cut the avenue verges and 500 yards of woodland paths using rotary cutter blades. Sue mowed banks and shrubberies with the strimmer and Flymo. The Atco mower made stripes on the lawn for special

Cutting grass

events. Two chainsaws and a leafblower were in regular use.

Cutting and raking long grass was a major task requiring all hands. There were 14 bins for leaf mould and compost. Weed control required Stephen vigilance while Andrew sprayed roses, maintained the avenue, gates and sheds and cleared mountains of fallen leaves. Each winter, damaged verges on the avenue needed frequent repairs to level up the broken turf.

Going Public

On a sunny day in May 1984 Sandy and Sue had a new experience when the fields and lawns at Ballindalloch erupted with pipers and side shows, a balloon race, pony rides, football, a model railway through the orchard and teas in the Ruin. That garden fete for Balfron Church was the first of ten big public events, and every single one of

them was blessed with good weather.

In 1987 the garden was fenced against deer and rabbits. Once the last offenders had been dispatched the place took on a new lease of life so Ballindalloch was opened for Scotland's Gardens Scheme in 1990. Like other new openers, Sandy and Sue were apprehensive. Julie Edmonstone was the Stirling organizer, deftly distributing sheaves of yellow notices. With words of wisdom she counselled 'Opening

Andrew's transport service

Plant stall for Scotland's Garden Scheme

Teas by Balfron WRI

your garden is like dying at dawn. It concentrates the mind wonderfully'.

After frantic preparations, displaying road signs and posters, hiring tables and crockery and persuading friends to help, the garden was opened for Riding for the Disabled, of which Sandy was the Honorary Treasurer. That day the sun shone ceaselessly on Ballindalloch while it rained everywhere else, including Balfron. The WRI served home-baked teas and a neighbour kindly commented 'What a lovely event for the village', Sue's mother said 'How nice it is to see all our friends' and a small cousin anxiously inquired 'Mummy, are *all* these people my relations?'

After that, Ballindalloch garden openings were announced in the Yellow Book about every third year and the Royal

National Lifeboat Institution was also supported. Sandy learned to station himself near the Actinidia *kolomikta* which climbed all over the south wall of the house displaying tri-coloured leaves which looked as if they had been dipped in pink and white paint. It never failed to draw enquiries and he could then oblige by identifying the only plant whose name he could remember. Sometimes 500 people arrived and one opening raised £3,000. Organizing openings meant weeks of extra work but thanks to wonderful helpers these efforts were fun and immensely rewarding.

Storm Damage

In 1992 foresters part felled and replanted the Village Strip and the Avenue Wood which the home team had just finished

Storm damage transformed the jungle .... and the lawn

clearing when a vicious gale prostrated another 40 big trees. It was an awesome prospect with the garden scheduled to open in two months but the Holmes, Scrimgeour and Brown families gallantly came to the rescue by sawing, clearing and burning it all until Ballindalloch was fit to welcome visitors. At the last minute, an aged laburnum keeled over in the garden. There was no time left for repairs so Sue hung up a notice saying 'Climbing Frame'.

Fatalities among the tree population were an annual occurrence. Sandy spent a whole winter demolishing two huge fallen beeches on the avenue and the log pile became monumental.

Zannah's Glen

The Avenue Wood was a major project. After felling and clearing, weeds sprang up but once the brambles, nettles, thistles, rushes and willow herb were held at bay, drifts of bluebells and foxgloves began to appear while irises, king cups and forget-me-nots came to edge the Clachan Burn. Before long Sandy was building bridges and steps while Sue began weaving a network of paths. By this time Susannah had qualified as a landscape architect and was able to help plan the planting so it became Zannah's Glen and soon the team was devoting as much time to the eleven acre wood as it did to the three acre garden. The glen called for rhododendrons so new specimens were planted and while the young trees were growing up it made a wonderful playground for children with

a bridge for 'Pooh Sticks' and a dog walking path which was named the K9.

Celebrations and Memorials

Special features commemorate people and events. Wild cherry trees on the avenue honour Sue's godmother, Marion (Silvia) Burrell. A whitebeam at the South Lodge

Terrace steps with Rose Felicia, Hosta Siebaldiana and clipped Box

Fiona and foxgloves in Zannah's Glen

'Funday' 2003 with some of the Classic Cars on parade.

celebrates John Ford's appointment as Deacon Convenor of the Trades House. An autumn flowering cherry tree was a thank you present from Zannah and Sacha after their dance. Later, red oaks were planted in the House Field and a little garden with stepping stones was made in memory of Sacha. In the paddock a grove of white cherry trees and narcissus celebrates the marriage of Graham and Trix. The births of three grand-daughters gave rise to Jessica's Meadow, Fiona's Steps and Melanie's Walk. To remember Zannah, a rustic seat was built in her glen. Although the Stephen's first daughter never lived at Ballindalloch a path along the Clachan

Burn was named Alice Way. In memory of their three daughters, Sue planted snowdrops along the verges and river bank near the entrance to Ballindalloch and, on the stone wall by the road approaching Balfron, the names and dates of Alice, Susannah (Zannah) and Alexandra (Sacha) are recorded on a small bronze plaque.

Final Fling

Ballindalloch seemed to thrive on gatherings so there were house parties, coach parties, pictics, barbecues, 'daffodil walks' and clay pigeon shoots. Meanwhile, developments continued, jungles were tamed, and more trees and shrubs planted. Even the dog kennel was given a garden. As frequent watering was required Sandy, as a present to Sue, spent a winter laying 70 yards of pipe-line. Some big stones were still lying about so he spent another winter constructing a 'prehistoric stone circle' at the bottom of the garden. An altar stone was considered, but the prospect of sacrificing a virgin seemed rather remote.

In their garden, Sandy and Sue tried to create atmosphere and encourage exploration, while hoping their develop-ments would evolve without too much evidence of human intervention. Sue liked to naturalize plants in unusual places and was pleased if they seemed to have got there on their own. The garden was the plants' domain so she tried to make them feel at home, but a firm hand was still needed because too much freedom can lead to delinquency. Sometimes, if the ground was dry, she entertained less agile guests by driving them round the garden walks in her car.

To autograph some of their innova-tions a cipher was made using two outlines of the letter S facing in opposite directions. It was carved by James Innes above the front door, on the entrance to the Ruin and also on a pair of folly gate posts in the garden. In the Ruin Garden a

stone seat was built and inscribed to mark the site of the Bronze Age tumulus.

It was a sad blow when Andrew Brown became ill in 2002 and had to give up his job at Ballindalloch. He was greatly missed by the Stephen household and the team was badly depleted without him. For over a year Sandy and Sue soldiered on without emplying further help until Malcolm Gillies came to work in the garden on Monday mornings and Betty Dunsmuir arrived to help in the house.

Balfron 700

When Balfron celebrated the village's 700th anniversary in 2003 a final fete was held at Ballindalloch. Its success was due to a big hearted team of enthusiasts who organized the show and transformed the gardens into a fairground of noise and colour with stalls, side shows and five marquees. A 1960s Bluebird motor coach came out of retirement to shuttle villagers from Balfron and fans arrived from near and far to see a cavalcade of 40 Classic motor cars. Sandy and Sue laid on an exhibition entitled 'The Lost History of Ballindalloch'. There were presentations and photos with the Provost of Stirling. The sun shone yet again and 1,100 people came to enjoy the biggest event the Stephens had ever hosted.

Golden Farewell

In 2004 Sandy and Sue celebrated their Golden Wedding. It was an anniversary they had hardly dared to anticipate and Sue nearly wrecked it by landing herself with a slipped disc through strimming a very steep bank. Mercifully, she managed

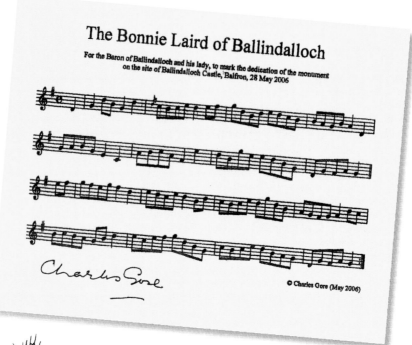

The Bonnie Laird of Ballindalloch

For the Baron of Ballindalloch and his lady, to mark the dedication of the monument
on the site of Ballindalloch Castle, Balfron, 28 May 2006

© Charles Gore (May 2006)

to get on her feet just in time for the party. Over the years she and Sandy sustained numerous horticultural injuries, but now they were in their seventies and beginning wear out. Having devoted half a lifetime to Ballindalloch it was difficult to stop. They were determined to open the garden just one more time. Being 'Open by Arrangement' was a new experience and after all the big events it was fun having time to chat with fellow enthusiasts. Sandy and Sue could not help feeling chuffed when a visitor said she liked their garden because 'Every corner is loved'.

Sandy longed for 'just another twenty five years', but all good things must come to an end. They loved the place too much to let it run down so in 2005 they agreed

Tai-haku, the great white cherry of Japan

Stone Circle

Bluebell Walk

West Lawn

View from the kitchen door

New rhododendrons

to sell the estate and move out the following year. They were glad that during the previous thirty years Ballindalloch had welcomed approximately 12,000 visitors.[4]

The Monument

As a parting gift Sandy and Sue commissioned a monument to mark the site of Ballindalloch Castle.[5] George Macmillan of Macmillan kindly donated the stone ball which stands on top. It had been part of an obsolete gateway from his home at Finlaystone which had once been the seat of the Earls of Glencairn. In May 2006 friends gathered to celebrate the unveiling. The object proved awkward to wrap, but three sheets and some string did the job.

George made a masterly speech and the three Stephen grand-daughters disrobed the monument. Charlie Gore brought his fiddle and completed the occasion by playing 'The Bonnie Laird of Ballindalloch' which he had composed, at Sue's request, as her birthday present to Sandy. There was much merriment and the 'Boney' laird was delighted. After all those sunny events the weather finally broke and the ceremony took place under a sea of coloured umbrellas. The company soon escaped indoors to dry out with reviving libations.

In June 2006 Sandy and Sue bade farewell to their beloved home and departed. It was a happy ending.

Remember this place

Epilogue

The ageing Stephens moved half a mile to the the edge of Balfron and settled happily in the little house where their cousin Johan Dunlop had ended her days.

Ballindalloch was bought by Tim and Sophie Trafford. Sophie's parents, James and Fiona Stirling of Garden, had long been friends of the Stephens, and James had played a major part in helping them find Ballindalloch thirty years before. Tim and Sophie are more than equal to the challenges ahead. In 1986 Sophie, with two of her friends, raised nearly £60,000 for cancer research by cycling from Cape Horn to Alaska. Since then Tim and

Sophie have voyaged to Antarctica in a yacht. At home, they are hands on, country people and dedicated gardeners, so their three young children will have a wonderful place in which to grow up.

Sandy and Sue enjoyed adapting the estate for modern times and hope that it will always be cherished. Over the years, the enchantment of Ballindalloch never ceased and they were aware of unseen forces near at hand. If the spirits of our Bronze Age forebears still roam these woods and fields, may they be at peace, knowing their sacred burial place is now a much loved garden.

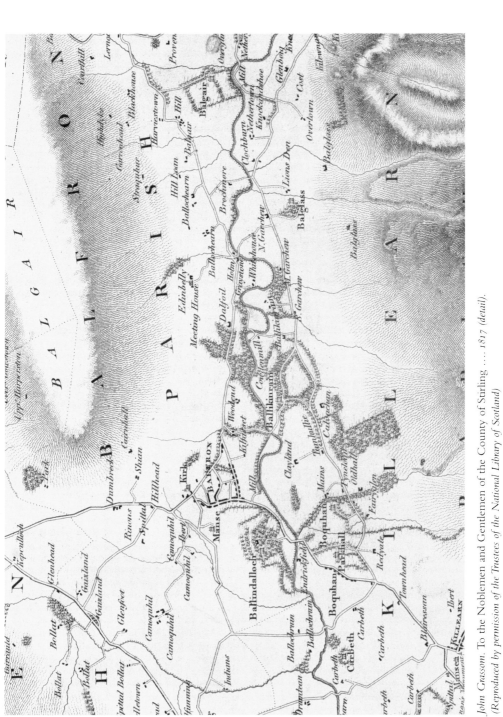

John Grassom. To the Noblemen and Gentlemen of the County of Stirling ..... 1817 (detail).
(Reproduced by permission of the Trustees of the National Library of Scotland)

Notes

INTRODUCTION
1. Charters of Inchaffrey Abbey CXIX
2. *Memoir of the Author* by Colin Dunlop Donald Note p. vii

CHAPTER 1: THE VANISHING TOWER AND THE MYSTERY MOUND
1. A fortalice is a fortified building.
2. Stirling Council Sites Monuments Record
3. J D Mackie *A History of Scotland.* 1964
4. Timothy Pont, who became a clergyman in Sutherland, did not live to see his monumental work published but Joan (pronounced Johan) Bleau published the survey in *Scotia Antiqva* in 1662. Other 'three turret' castles within 10 miles of Ballindalloch were Bardowy, Buchanan, Coulknock (Culcreugh), Gartnefs, and Kylmaronok.
5. Rev. William Nimmo *History of Stirlingshire*

CHAPTER 2: THE BRONZE AGE
1. c.2500 BC building in stone began at Stonehenge Francis Pryor *Britain BC* p.238. c.2000 BC Abraham's journey *Good News Bible.* c.1200 Fall of Troy
2. Royal Commission of the Ancient and Historical Monuments of Scotland
3. Colin Burgess *The Age of Stonehenge* p.324
4. Andreas Boos *Gods and Heroes of the European Bronze Age* 1998 p.106
5. Homer, Greek epic poet 8th century BC, related traditional stories. Although many characters may be fictional, evidence still exists at Mycenae, Pylos and Troy

6. Colin Burgess *The Age of Stonehenge* 1980 p.89
7. Ibid p.62
8. Ibid p.79
9. Ibid p.195
10. Ibid p.162
11. Francis Pryor, *Britain BC* 2003 p.296

CHAPTER 3: THE DARK AGES OF BALLINDALLOCH
1. Colin Burgess *The Age of Stonehenge* p.156
2. Francis Pryor *Britain BC* 2003 p.236
3. Colin Burgess *The Age of Stonehenge* 1980 p.165
4. The Royal Commission on Ancient and Historical Monuments in Scotland *Stirlingshire* Vol. 1
5. Robert Lacey and Danny Danziger *The Year 1000* 2000 p.136
6. J Guthrie Smith *The Parish of Strathblane* 1886 p.9
7. *Burke's Peerage and Baronetage 1926*
8. Ibid. The Earls of Perth
9. *The Genealogy of the House of Drummond* p.38
10. *Burke's Peerage and Baronetage 1926*, The Earls of Perth
11. Marc Morris *The Castle* 2003
12. The Motte is described in Gifford and Walker's *Stirling and Central Scotland, Buildings of Scotland* as 'MOTTE, Woodend, 1km SE of Clachan. Readily defensible natural mound, c.3m. high, flattened on top to form an oval platform 40m. by 34m'.
13. J Guthrie Smith *Strathendrick and its Inhabitants from early times* 1896 pps.38, 39–40
14. J D Mackie *A History of Scotland* 1964 p.53
15. *Cart. De Lennox, 67*

CHAPTER 4: THE CUNNINGHAM EARLS OF GLENCAIRN

1. Though spelling varies 'Cunningham' has been used through most of the book
2. Cal. Doc. Scot. ii 212, Palgrave, 308, 314
3. Papal Registers, Petitions, i 639
4. Kilkerran Family Papers
5. Reg. Mag. Sig.
6. Acta Parl. Scot. ii 450
7. Statistical Account of Scotland 1841
8. Foedora xv 23
9. *Winning Tales from Scottish Houses* George and Jane MacMillan 1986 The Family Tree
10. P.C.Reg. iii 506, 509
11. *Winning Tales from Scottish Houses* George and Jane MacMillan 1986 The Family Tree
12. Acta Parl. Scot. vii 44, 277
13. Nicoll's Diary
14. High Treasurer's Accounts, I 9
15. P.C. Reg. iii 1
16. P.C. Reg. iv 256
17. Douglas *The Scots Peerage*. Cunningham, Earl of Glencairn
18. *Winning Tales from Scottish Houses* George and Jane MacMillan 1986 The Family Tree
19. Douglas *The Scots Peerage*

CHAPTER 5: THE CUNNINGHAMS OF BALLINDALLOCH

1. J Guthrie Smith *The Parish of Strathblane* 1886 p.88
2. Cart de Lennox, 67
3. Timothy Pont *Cunninghame Topographied* pub.1876 with additions by James Dobie p.167–8
4. The engraving of Glengarnock Castle is reproduced from Pont and Dobbie *Cunninghame Topographied 1876* and the plan from David McGibbon and Thomas Ross *Castellated and Domestic Architecture of Scotland* Vol. 3 p.293.
5. J Guthrie Smith *The Parish of Strathblane* p.229
6. Ibid p.105
7. Douglas *The Scots Peerage* Cunningham p.230
8. J Guthrie Smith *The Parish of Strathblane* p.309
9. Douglas *The Scots Peerage* Cunningham p.245
10. J Guthrie Smith *The Parish of Strathblane* 1886 pps.87–88
11. The Petition of Janet Mitchell relict of James Kay and Thomas Kay brother of James Kay 12 Feb 1751

12. Royal Commission of Ancient and Historical Monuments of Scotland *Stirlingshire* Vol. 1 Stirlingshire p.367
13. J Guthrie Smith *Strathendrick and its Inhabitants from early times* 1896 p.263
14. Robert Louis Stevenson *Kidnapped*, chapter XX

CHAPTER 6: BARONS AND BARONIES

1. Charters were sometimes granted by an Earl but the Ballindalloch charters were direct from the King.
2. David M Walker *A Legal History of Scotland*. The Author confesses that he too does not fully understand the meanings of these words.
3. Charters were dated 21 April 1599, 12 February 1613, 26 June 1613, 22 July 1613, 20 December 1622, 24 June 1646 and 17 June 1687.
4. In Perthshire these are not known but a Kildinny near Forgandenny still exists.

CHAPTER 7: ROBERT DUNMORE

1. Guthrie Smith. Mitchell & Buchanan *The Old Country Houses of the Old Gentry* 1878
2. Ibid.
3. The Royal Commission of the Ancient & Historical Monuments of Scotland, *Stirlingshire* Vol. 2
4. Dunmore's developments in Balfron have been recorded by Jim Thomson in *The Balfron Heritage*, 1991
5. Statistical Account of Scotland 1791–99
6. Ibid. 1841
7. Ibid 1791–99
8. J Guthrie Smith *Strathendrick and its Inhabitants from early times* 1896 p.205
9. When Sandy and Sue arrived at Ballindalloch in 1976, Sandy's cousin William Cuthbert and his wife Caroline were living at Old Ballikinrain, and the two households enjoyed a neighbourly connection for many years.
10. It is understood that there are Dunmore papers still in existence.

CHAPTER 8: THE COOPER FAMILY

1. Failford near Mauchline had originally been a Priory. According to Douglas, *The Scottish Peerage* during the 16th century Robert Cunningham of Montgrenane, 4th son of the

5th Earl of Glencairn was minister [*sic*] of the Priory of Failford.

During the 20th century Failford was owned by Sandy Stephen's great uncle, another Alexander Stephen.

2. Burke *The Landed Gentry of Great Britain*
3. Cooper letters
4. J Guthrie Smith *Strathendrick and its Inhabitants from early times* 1896 p.49
5. Cooper letters

CHAPTER 9: THE DONALDSON FAMILY

1. Balfunning House, built in 1884, is two miles west of Ballindalloch, just off the A811.
2. Aucheneden is off the Stockiemuir Road, just south of the Queen's View.
3. Minter letter 4/9/1986.
4. When the house was being dismantled, prior to demolition, invitations and postcards were discovered behind the servants' hall mantelpiece, along with other items which must have slipped down the back.
5. St Hilda's school was evacuated from Liberton near Edinburgh and Sue Stephen (*nee* Thomson) spent nearly two years there during WWII.
6. Winston Churchill *The Second World War* Vol. II p.276.
7. Camoquhill Douglas is now owned by John Denholm, Sandy Stephen's nephew.

CHAPTER 10: THE GLEN FAMILY

1. Sir William Burrell's only child Marion, who later changed her name to Silvia, was Sue Stephen's godmother.
2. Richard Marks. *Burrell* 1883 p.150

CHAPTER 11: THE STEPHEN FAMILY

1. John Gifford and Frank Arneil Walker, *The Buildings of Scotland; Stirling and Central Scotland*, 2001. Page 191/2 describes the house:

'BALLINDALLOCH, 1.2 km W [of Balfron]. A charming one-and-a-half storey, crowstep-gabled, three bay house reconstituted from fragments of its predecessor by naval architect *Alexander Stephen*, 1978–9. … In 1868–9 this first dwelling was replaced by a two-storey-and attic, mildly Scots mansion designed by *David Thomson*, of which elements have been creatively conscripted to architectural service in the present more modest house. Of three gabled dormers on the s front only one is in its original position (part of the old services wing). Bold roll-moulded details reincorporated at window and door jambs.

A delightful garden to the s is romantically enhanced by the retention of ruinous bay-windowed walling from the C19 mansion. C17 obelisk SUNDIAL'.

CHAPTER 12: THE GOOD LIFE

1. Few flagstones were lifted. The large ones were shifted using levers and rollers.
2. Narcissus *Val Sion*
3. Gifford & Walker *The Buildings of Scotland; Stirling and Central Scotland*, 2001. Describes the South Lodge as '0.7km. SW [of Balfron], immediately N of Field Bridge. By *Launcelot H. Ross*. Dated 1924 over pedimented door. Crowstep gables and pedimented eaves dormers: suburban sub-Baronial in cream roughcast with red sandstone dressings'.
4. Estimate from Sue's diary records. Besides shooting, tennis and visits from friends at least 17 charities and societies were supported.
5. The Monument, the Ruin Seat and the Folly Gate were constructed and carved by James Innes & Son, Stonemasons, of Doune. SMOS designed the monument.